GREAT
ANCIENT
CHINA
PROJECTS

LANCE KRAMER
ILLUSTRATED BY STEVEN WEINBERG

green press INITIATIVE

Nomad Press is committed to preserving ancient forests and natural resources. We elected to print *Great Ancient China Projects* on 30% postconsumer recycled paper, processed chlorine free. As a result, for this printing, we have saved:

24 Trees (40' tall and 6-8" diameter)
8,654 Gallons of Wastewater
586 Kilowatt Hours of Electricity
1,111 Pounds of Solid Waste
2,085 Pounds of Greenhouse Gases

Nomad Press made this paper choice because our printer, Sheriden, is a member of Green Press Initiative, a non-profit program dedicated to supporting authors, publishers, and suppliers in their efforts to reduce their use of fiber obtained from endangered forests.

For more information, visit www.greenpressinitiative.org

Illustrations by Steven Weinberg

Questions regarding the ordering of this book should be addressed to
Independent Publishers Group
814 N. Franklin St.
Chicago, IL 60610
www.ipgbook.com

Nomad Press
2456 Christian St.
White River Junction, VT 05001

CONTENTS

Timeline ◙ iv

Introduction ◙ 1

A Civilization Like
None Other ◙ 4

Cities and Architecture ◙ 8

Paper ◙ 16

Writing and
Education ◙ 22

Warriors and
Weapons ◙ 30

Jade and Silk ◙ 43

Merchants and Trade ◙ 48

Explorers and Sailing ◙ 58

Healers and Medicine ◙ 66

Farming ◙ 72

Food ◙ 80

Time and Space ◙ 91

Music ◙ 97

Chang Heng's
Seismograph ◙ 104

Numbers ◙ 108

Glossary   Resources   Index

TIMELINE

Most historians break China's history up into the following dynasties, or periods of time, when a family or group of people ruled over China. BCE after a date stands for Before Common Era and counts down to zero. CE stands for Common Era and counts up from zero. These are non-religious terms corresponding to BC and AD.

中國古代
ANCIENT CHINA

SHANG DYNASTY - 1600 TO 1046 BCE

- The emergence of the earliest formal Chinese state. Writing is established and a military developed. Shang settlements are constantly at war with neighboring peoples and villages.

- Archaeologists have discovered wheels in China dating back to at least 1500 BCE.

WESTERN ZHOU DYNASTY - 1046 TO 771 BCE

- The Zhou kings conquer the Shang state in the middle of the eleventh century BCE.

EASTERN ZHOU DYNASTY - 770 TO 256 BCE

- Small sections of fortified walls are built by various feudal states.

- Once armies adopt the idea of a cavalry from the nomads, military strength grows to over 100,000 men.

SPRING AND AUTUMN PERIOD - 770 TO 476 BCE

- Confucius, one of the most important thinkers in Chinese history, lives from 551 to 479 BCE. His teachings influence much of Chinese education and many beliefs and customs even today.

- In the sixth century BCE, Sun Tzu writes the famous war philosophy text, *The Art of War.*

- Kites are invented in China during the fifth century BCE.

- The Chinese invent the farming hoe between the fifth and sixth centuries BCE.

WARRING STATES PERIOD - 475 TO 221 BCE

- Bronze coins from ancient China date back to the fifth century BCE.

- Relief maps are used for records and navigation as early as the third century BCE.

TIMELINE

QIN DYNASTY – 221 TO 207 BCE

- Emperor Qin Shi Huangdi, or the "First Emperor," takes power in 221 BCE. He begins to join together existing city walls and construct the Great Wall along the empire's northern borders.
- The emperor unifies Chinese script and tears down walls between states.
- The Terracotta Army is buried with Emperor Shi Huangdi between 210 and 209 BCE.

WESTERN HAN DYNASTY – 206 BCE TO 23 CE

- The Han Dynasty expands the roles of the emperor and creates a permanent army.
- Ts'ai Lun, an official in the imperial court, is believed to invent paper in 105 BCE.
- By 200 BCE, the crossbow is a common weapon used by Chinese soldiers.
- The Han Dynasty is the first to standardize weights and measurements.
- The Chinese astronomer Keng Shou-Ch'ang invents the first armillary sphere in 52 BCE to help measure the stars and planets.

EASTERN HAN DYNASTY – 25 TO 220 CE

- By the end of the second century CE, China already has more than 22,000 miles of roads.
- The wheelbarrow is first used in China in the first century CE.
- The first Chinese junk, or sailboat, is developed around 200 CE.
- In 132 CE, scientist, inventor, mathematician, and royal astronomer Chang Heng invents the first seismograph to predict earthquakes.

THE THREE KINGDOMS – 220 TO 265 CE

- After the Han Dynasty collapses, three rival kingdoms take control and create great unrest.

THE PERIOD OF DISUNION – 265 TO 618 CE

- Around 600 CE, the city of Xi'an has more than one million people living inside its walls, making it the largest city in the world.
- Around 350 CE, farmers begin to cultivate tea.

TIMELINE

THE TANG DYNASTY - 618 TO 907 CE

- The first experiments with fireworks take place in 850 CE.
- During the seventh century, the Chinese begin construction of the Grand Canal, the largest ancient canal in the world.

THE FIVE DYNASTIES - 907 TO 960 CE

- The Chinese invent gate locks, making travel along canals much easier and more efficient.

NORTHERN SONG DYNASTY - 960 TO 1126 CE

- In 1041 CE, a man named Bi Sheng makes the first moveable type apparatus.
- By the eleventh century, Chinese coins are used as a common currency throughout Asia.
- In 1040 CE, the first magnetic compass is invented.
- Su Song invents his famous mechanical clock in 1092 CE.
- Changes in government policy and advances in printing technology lead to better education, literacy, and access to books.

SOUTHERN SONG DYNASTY - 1127 TO 1279 CE

- The naval technology of the Song Dynasty helps defend the empire from foreign invasions, especially the Mongols, for a century.

YUAN (MONGOL) DYNASTY - 1279 TO 1368 CE

- After many bloody and violent battles, Mongolians take control of China and divide the country, often based on ethnicity.
- Beijing becomes the new capital of China when Khubilai Khan, the first Mongol emperor, builds his imperial city there.

MING DYNASTY - 1368 TO 1644 CE

- Most construction of the Great Wall takes place between 1368 and 1644 CE.
- The Forbidden City is built in Beijing between 1406 and 1420 CE and serves as the imperial palace until 1912 CE.
- The great Chinese explorer Zheng He is born in 1371 CE. Zheng travels to Asia, India, the Persian Gulf, Arabia, Africa, and the Americas with a fleet of ships and crews of more than 20,000 men.

INTRODUCTION

In today's world, teachers in the United States and Europe usually teach only one subject. Your science teacher might only teach science. Or your history teacher might only teach history. But in ancient China, the best scholars, or wise people, had more than one specialty. It was not enough to be an expert in history or science. A wise person also had to be able to paint, to write in **calligraphy**, and maybe even play a musical instrument.

Some scholars wrote poetry while others trained to become expert archers. Some were even warriors who understood military tactics. And there was also a good chance they knew about farming techniques. It sure took a lot to rise to the top of ancient Chinese society and get some respect!

Chinese compass from 200 BCE

This book will show you how to become a modern "wise person." You'll explore the many different parts of ancient China. You'll learn about each of the major dynasties throughout its history. You'll find out what it was like to be the ruler of the whole Chinese Empire. And you'll learn about important Chinese thinkers, such as **Confucius**. Even more than 1,000 years after his death, Chinese people today still follow his ideas. You'll discover how people made things like bronze casts and porcelain pottery. Finally, you'll read the amazing stories behind some of ancient China's most important inventions, such as paper, moveable type, the magnetic compass, gunpowder, and even the world's first kite.

Many of these inventions changed the world. But they did not come from famous inventors, such as Thomas Edison or Leonardo da Vinci. Usually, inventions came from ordinary people who wanted to solve an everyday problem. For example, **nomads** invented stirrups because they spent most of their time traveling on horseback. They were just looking for a way to make riding a horse easier! A printer invented moveable type because he wanted a way to make his job go more quickly.

Throughout this book, you will have the chance to build your own version of lots of these inventions. For most projects, you won't even have to go to the store to buy materials. Instead, you will be able to use things you can find right in your home. You'll learn to appreciate the amazing creativity of ancient Chinese thinkers. You'll discover many things about different parts of Chinese history and culture. And, best of all, you'll have your own working models of some of the most famous Chinese inventions. These inventions may even inspire you to think of ideas that can improve things in your own life and the world around you.

游牧人
NOMADS

WORDS TO KNOW

calligraphy: the art of beautiful writing.

Confucius: a wise man and one of the most famous thinkers in ancient China. He lived from 551 to 479 BCE.

nomads: people that move from one place to another, instead of living in one place.

書法
CALLIGRAPHY

A CIVILIZATION LIKE NONE OTHER

About 1.3 billion people live in China, out of the 6.7 billion people alive in the world today. Think about it. This means that almost one out of every five people in the world live in China. China is about the same size as the United States, but there are more than four times as many people living there!

China is one of the largest and most important countries in the world. It's also one of the oldest. Chinese history began at least 5,000 years ago and continues right up to today. Other ancient nations, such as ancient Rome or Egypt, have risen and fallen. But Chinese society and culture has continued to grow since the first rulers, called the Shang **Dynasty**, took power in 1600 BCE.

朝代

DYNASTY

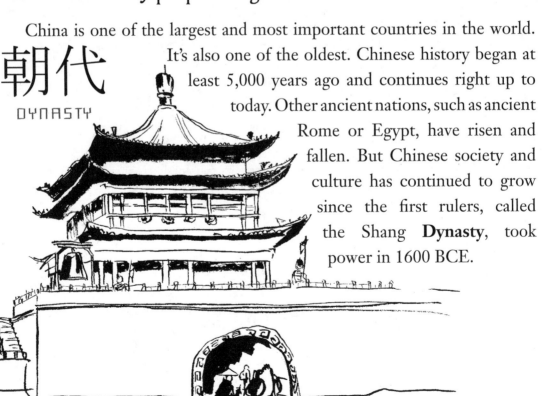

天命
MANDATE
OF HEAVEN

This was almost 200 years before King Tut ruled Egypt, and over 3,000 years before America's Declaration of Independence was signed. Today, China is home to many different people, cultures, religions, and even languages. It is experiencing many different changes. But it's amazing how so many Chinese people still look back to their ancient history. They take great pride in their ancient traditions, which still remain important in daily life.

Ancient China was a fascinating place in which to live, with a reputation as one of the most advanced and important places in the known world. In 1000 BCE, the Zhou kings called China "The Middle Kingdom" because they believed China was the center of the world! They also thought that China was the middle point between humans on earth and the gods in the heavens. Therefore, the Chinese believed that the emperor had a direct connection to the gods, called a **Mandate of Heaven**. This special relationship helped him to gain the trust and respect of his people.

China has always been, and still is, mostly a rural country. This means that most Chinese people live and work in the countryside on farms. But ancient China was also home to some of the largest and most advanced cities on earth. For example, in the seventh century (600 CE), the city of Xi'an had more than one million people living inside its walls. At the time, it was the largest city in the world.

China's cities brought together some of the world's most brilliant thinkers. They had lots of new ideas about art, science, writing,

WORDS TO KNOW

dynasty: a powerful family or group that rules for many years. Some ancient Chinese dynasties continued for several hundred years and some were very short.

Mandate of Heaven: the idea that China's emperor got his power straight from heaven. That meant people trusted him to rule over their lives.

monastery: a place where monks devoted their lives to prayer and religious study.

and government. Chinese architects designed many wonders of the world. These include the Great Wall of China, a magnificent army of lifesize clay warriors, and the huge Imperial City in Beijing, with over 900 separate buildings inside its walls. They also built hundreds of beautiful temples and **monasteries** throughout the country.

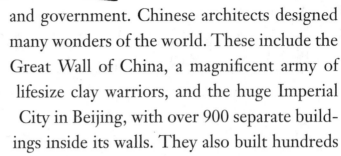

寺院
MONASTERY

Ancient China didn't have telephones, airplanes, or the Internet. But the Chinese found many ways to stay closely connected with other people. The Silk Road brought together merchants and travelers from many parts of the world. This road started as a way for merchants to sell goods. In addition to carrying pottery, jade, silk, and tea, merchants also carried new information about mathematics, astronomy, and religion. People were able to exchange ideas, inventions, and stories about new places. The Silk Road helped thousands of people communicate and understand the world.

For about 2,500 years, many people considered the area known as the North China Plain to be the center of China. This is where the Shang Dynasty came into being between 1600 and 1045 BCE. A thousand years later, China's realm extended from the area of Sichuan in the southwestern part of the country all the way to the South China Sea. To the north, the kingdom's dominion ran all the way to the central Asian grasslands. To the west, China's borders included the Himalaya Mountains. And to the south, they covered the high Tibetan Plateau. In the far north, just below Mongolia, is the vast and arid Gobi Desert. In the far south, the area around the Pearl River is home to a dense rain forest. The current borders of China have not changed much since the Qing dynasty in the eighteenth century.

China possesses some of the most spectacular and diverse landscapes in the world. There are high, rugged mountains and deep, bending river valleys. In fact, China is home to several of the world's longest and most important rivers. The Yangzi River is the third-longest river in the world, after the Amazon River in South America and the Nile River in Egypt. The Yangzi flows for nearly 4,000 miles and divides the north and south of China. Another famous river is the Yellow River. It runs through the Gobi Desert in the north before emptying into the Yellow Sea. The mountains and rivers of China have played an important role in the development of China. They've also been the subject for all different kinds of Chinese art, especially painting.

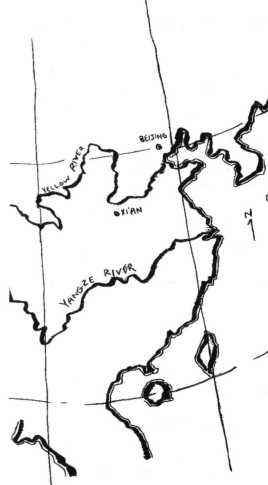

POLLUTION IN CHINA

Although China is full of natural beauty, it's also home to some of the world's worst pollution. China has grown tremendously in recent years. The cars and factories in its enormous cities produce thick smog, which is unhealthy to breathe. Many of China's once dense forests have been cut down to make way for farms and cities. Pollution in China doesn't only affect the Chinese. Scientists have found Chinese pollution hundreds, and sometimes even thousands, of miles from China's borders. It's important to everyone that China works to save its land and keep its people healthy.

CITIES AND ARCHITECTURE

Imagine living in a city with over one million people inside four giant walls that run more than 20 miles around! That's what it was like inside the imperial capital city of Xi'an in 600 CE. At the time, Xi'an was the final stop on the Silk Road. It was also one of the largest cities in the world.

Until the twentieth century, the Chinese built a wall around almost every one of their cities. They made the walls from **rammed earth**. At first, walls were a way to protect the city from outside invaders. But even after walls were no longer a good defense, they remained an important symbol of ancient Chinese cities.

THE GREAT WALL

The most famous wall in China is the Great Wall. Most people agree that the Emperor Qin Shi Huangdi (pronounced "chin shee-hwang-dee") was the ruler who first began building the wall. Some portions of the wall had been built as early as 700 BCE but Shi Huangdi joined the sections and greatly expanded the wall starting in 221 BCE. The emperor believed that the Great Wall would keep out China's barbarian neighbors to the north. Even more of the Great Wall was built between 1368 and 1644 CE under the Ming Dynasty. At one point, the Great Wall stretched over 1,600 miles. Unfortunately, much of the wall is now in ruins. But since UNESCO declared it a **World Heritage Site** in 1987, major parts of it have been restored to their original beauty.

Cities were the center for government and trade in ancient China. The market, or *shicheng*, was located in the middle of the

WORDS TO KNOW

rammed earth: a building process that involves compressing a mixture of sand, gravel, and clay into a solid wall.

apothecaries: ancient pharmacies selling medicine and herbs.

UNESCO: a United Nations organization that helps preserve historic and ancient sites.

World Heritage Site: a special place named by UNESCO that deserves to be restored or preserved, like the Great Wall of China.

city. The *shicheng* was one of the few open areas in the city. Farmers came to the *shicheng* to trade their grain and produce. Silversmiths, embroiderers, tailors, and other craftsmen also sold their handiwork at the market. People could buy medicine and herbs in the market's **apothecaries**.

The palace was also located near the heart of the city. The palace was like a city inside a city. It had its own gardens, temples, and monasteries. Government

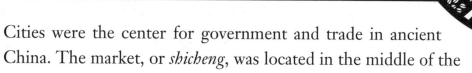

寺院
COMMERCE

offices were here too. The palace showed off the emperor's power and authority. A magnificent palace reminded the people of his connection to heaven.

The most famous Chinese palace still standing is the Forbidden City in Beijing. It was built during the Ming and Qing Dynasties and has more than 800 buildings within its walls. It is called the Forbidden City because no one could enter or leave without the emperor's permission.

WORDS TO KNOW

symmetrical: a building or design that looks the same on both sides, like a mirror image.

asymmetrical: a design that does not look the same on both sides.

One of the most important contributions ancient China made to architecture was the innovative and creative ways they used wood. The Chinese were brilliant at building wooden interlocking joints. This allowed them to make frames that could support the heavy, sloped roofs that hang over the edge of walls. This style of building can be seen throughout China. Wooden buildings hold up very well during earthquakes, which are common in China. But they can also burn down easily if there is a fire.

Most buildings were lined up perfectly from north to south, like a compass. When it was possible, the Chinese designed buildings to be **symmetrical**. This meant they looked the same on both sides. This was true for everything except

gardens, which were supposed to be as **asymmetrical** as possible, or different on both sides. The Chinese thought of gardens as works of art that connected nature and the city.

Chinese architects always followed a sacred set of rules for building called *feng shui* (pronounced fang shway). These rules applied to both peasants and emperors. Feng shui means "wind and water," and it still has a great influence over life in China today.

FENG SHUI

Many Chinese believe that the earth, humans, and the heavens are all connected. What connects them is an invisible energy force they call *qi* (pronounced "chee"). In order to live a successful life, a person must allow this force to flow around him or her as much as possible. Feng shui is the practice of arranging objects and space to help with this flow.

FENG SHUI

According to the rules of feng shui, the perfect house would be in a beautiful spot with a view of the mountains to the rear and from both sides. The house might have a peaceful stream flowing right past the front door. Of course, not everyone could afford a house in the mountains. But those rich enough to design their own house would usually hire a feng shui expert. This person would make sure the house was built in such a way that the family inside would always prosper and have a healthy relationship with nature.

BUILD A 'MINI-YURT'

Different ethnic groups within China had their own unique building styles. For example, the nomadic Mongols often built yurts, which were rounded tents held up by a wooden pole framework. They were covered by skins and were easy to move.

Yurts were designed to be very portable and easy to build. Your "mini-yurt" might be a little too small to live in, but it should still give you a taste of what it was like to build one!

SUPPLIES

box of toothpicks

bag of marshmallows

pen or pencil

compass

cereal box

scissors

sewing needle

ruler

construction paper

colored pencils, crayons, or markers

wood glue

1 Arrange two groups of eight toothpicks, each in an octagon shape, like a stop sign. Use the marshmallows to connect the toothpicks at each joint on each octagon.

2 One of the octagons is your base. Take out another 8 toothpicks to be your "support posts." Connect them one by one to the marshmallows in the base so that they point upwards. Each support post should make a right angle with the base.

3 Attach the second octagon to the tops of the posts by poking the tops of the toothpicks through the marshmallows.

4 Now here's the tricky part—making the roof. This was also the trickiest part when making a real yurt. Take out eight more toothpicks to form the roof frame. Each toothpick will need to be angled in towards the center of the yurt but also up. One-by-one, attach toothpicks to the top marshmallow joints of the upper octagon frame, pointing inwards. Don't worry if they sag down a little bit—the next step will fix this.

5 Using your compass, measure out a circle with a 3½-inch diameter on your cereal box. If you don't have a compass, it's okay to draw a circle by hand.

6 Cut out the circle. Then draw another circle inside the one you've just cut out, with a diameter of 3 inches. Cut out the inner circle, so you're left with a ring. Use the sewing needle to poke eight holes in the ring, spaced out equally.

7 Take the ring and hold it up in the middle of the yurt's roof. This will be the main support for the roof and will serve as the smokehole (though you won't be burning any firewood inside yours!). If you've measured everything out correctly, you should be able to attach the roof toothpicks directly into the holes in the cardboard ring.

8 Here's your chance to personalize your yurt. A traditional yurt would be covered with the wool taken from its owner's flock of sheep. But unless you have your own flock of sheep, you'll probably have to use something like construction paper for the yurt covering! Measure the dimensions of one of the open-side faces of the yurt structure. Measure out a rectangle on your construction paper fitting those same dimensions. Cut the corners so that it will fit around the marshmallows.

9 Apply a thin layer of glue to the edges of the construction paper cutout. Attach it directly to the outer side toothpicks, so that it forms an outside wall. Repeat this step for all of the open faces. But be sure to leave one of the side faces open, otherwise you'll have no way to get inside!

BUILD A FENG SHUI

In this activity you'll design the ideal house according to feng shui rules. You can also reorganize your room using some of these ideas.

Stairs should never face the front door. So, when you are designing your house, make sure that the front door and stairway (if there are two floors in your house) are apart from each other. Roads in ancient China were always windy and curvy to keep away evil spirits, who could only travel in straight lines. If you would like to make a windy road leading up to your house, this will help to make your design have good feng shui and keep you safe from the evil spirits! Good feng shui means avoiding clutter and keeping things neat, which lets the energy flow harmoniously through your house. This might be hard to show in a drawing, but in your own house where you live now, you can start having good feng shui today by cleaning up your room!

SUPPLIES

pen or pencil

ruler

colored pencils

large paper with grid lines

1. The best shape for a house with good feng shui is a rectangle. First draw a large rectangle big enough to fit all the rooms and details inside. You can choose a "U" or "L" shape, but then you must add other natural elements (such as trees, a fountain, or a garden) to the border to close the open side. When you are finished, the outline of your house should have no openings. Use your ruler and follow the lines of your grid paper, so that you have a neat design with straight edges.

2. Divide the house into nine equal sections, or rooms and label them. Each room will be one of your nine *bagua* (pronounced "bag-wa"). In feng shui, each *bagua* is a different aspect of life. So each room in your house will represent a different part of your life. For example, if your family room is the "wisdom and knowledge" room, then this is the place where you should study and keep your books. The Chinese believed that keeping your nine *bagua* in harmony kept different parts of your life in harmony.

HOUSE

3 Choose where to place your front door. This is an important decision. The room you enter first in your house will determine which room, or bagua, is most important to you. For example, if you value health and family most, put the entrance in this room.

4 Choose which color each room will be. In Chinese culture and feng shui, each color has a different symbolic meaning or mood. To make good feng shui, you should use a mix of many different colors throughout the house to balance the *qi*. Here are some examples of the meanings of different colors:

red: attraction, warmth, strength. Red also means energy and too much can cause an argument. Use it sparingly.

orange: sense of purpose, organization.

blue: calm, relaxation.

green: health, potential.

purple: spiritual guidance.

yellow: energy, life.

pink: love, romance.

black: mood, perception, money. Too much black can be draining so only use it a little.

Nine *Bagua*

career	for grown-ups, this area refers to jobs. For children it refers to school.
wisdom and knowledge	learning, knowledge, and study.
health and family	physical and emotional health, as well as your ancestors, current family, friends, and co-workers.
wealth	money and anything else that makes you feel blessed.
fame and reputation	how the world sees you.
love and marriage	personal relationships, such as those between husband and wife, business partners, and good friends.
children and creativity	children, current projects, or anything creative.
helpful people	relationships with people other than your family and friends, such as a stranger who has touched your life, a mentor at work, your priest, or rabbi (or other spiritual guide).
center or *qi*	harmonizes all the areas together. It represents health and longevity and is the center of the *bagua*. It should be as uncluttered as possible.

DID YOU KNOW?

When building a house, feng shui practitioners even had to consider what time of day construction could take place. Some times were luckier than others!

PAPER

Look around the room you are in right now. You'll probably see at least one sheet of paper. It's everywhere! Paper is one of the most important inventions to come from ancient China.

The history of paper is complex. The word for "paper" actually comes from the word "papyrus." But papyrus is very different from the paper that we use today. Papyrus is made from the **fibers** of the papyrus plant and was first used in ancient Egypt five thousand years ago.

紙　絲
PAPER　FIBERS

The kind of paper we use today was invented in China during the second century BCE. Many historians say that the man who invented paper was named Ts'ai Lun. He was an official in the Chinese Imperial Court during the Han Dynasty. As the story goes, in the year 105 BCE, Ts'ai Lun brought the emperor samples of paper he had made. He had spent many years trying out different materials and processes.

As you can imagine, the process for making paper has changed since Ts'ai Lun's time. Nowadays, we make paper with wood. First the wood is ground up into very small pieces called fibers. This ground-up wood is called **wood pulp**.

The ancient Chinese made paper with fibers too, but their fibers didn't come from wood. Most likely they first tried breaking up old rags into fibers. Eventually, they began using fibers from bamboo, the mulberry tree, **hemp**, wheat stalks, and even rice. The bark of the mulberry tree was especially valuable and handy. The Chinese even used it to make paper clothing, hats, belts, and shoes!

DID YOU KNOW?

In 1957 archaeologists discovered one of the oldest pieces of paper in the world in a tomb near Xi'an. It was about 10 inches square. Archaeologists believe this piece of paper dates from sometime around 100 BCE.

The papermaker first separated the fibers, and mixed them together with water. The mixture was then laid into a flat mold. This mold had a mesh screen so that the excess water could drain away. The water that

TOILET PAPER

People in ancient China may have used paper for books and art. They also realized paper could be useful for other things. In particular, China was probably the first place to use toilet paper. Historical records show that toilet paper was used as early as the sixth century CE. In 1393 it was recorded that 720,000 large sheets of toilet paper were created for the Imperial Court. Each sheet was about 2 feet by 3 feet. The emperor used fancy toilet paper that was soft and perfumed. Guess you could say he was a pretty lucky guy!

remained helped the fibers to expand and hold together. Once everything dried, a thick, rough surface of paper was left on the mold. Then the piece of paper was usually hung to dry some more and the papermaker got ready to make his next piece!

The ancient Chinese depended on paper just as much as we do today. Scholars used paper to study and write. The government used paper to make records and issue orders. Merchants used paper to conduct daily business. And artists made beautiful prints and wrote in calligraphy on paper.

Though it's hard to imagine writing on anything else, many people in ancient China didn't use paper after it was invented. The first types of paper were very **coarse** and difficult to write on. So people tried writing on pottery, silk, and even turtle shells. Imagine having to do your homework on those!

WORDS TO KNOW

fibers: the smaller pieces or threads of a material that has been broken down.

wood pulp: a fluffy material that results when wood is broken down.

hemp: a plant that grows in Asia. Its fibers are used to make many materials.

coarse: a surface that feels harsh or rough to the touch.

MAKE YOUR OWN PAPER

SUPPLIES

material for fiber *(suggestions: computer paper, toilet paper, newspaper, construction paper, magazines, egg cartons, etc.)*

scissors

blender

water

flower heads, yarn, thread, or seeds for extra color or texture

foil brownie pan

window screening *(available at most hardware stores)*

rubber bands

flat plastic tub larger than the size of the brownie pan

sponge

dishtowel or old cloth

paper towels

rolling pin

Ts'ai Lun experimented with all kinds of different materials to make his paper. This shows that there is no one right way to make paper. Depending on which ingredients you use, there are a million and one different kinds of paper you can make. Here are just a few suggestions for materials to use for fiber. Don't be afraid to be creative and come up with something entirely new!

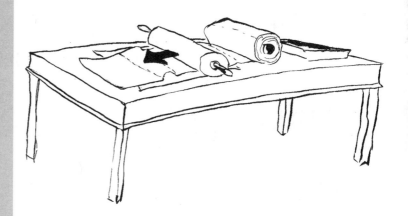

ᒪ PAPER

1 Cut or tear the material you've chosen for the fiber into smaller pieces. Each piece should be about one inch around. Fill the blender up to about the halfway mark with the torn pieces of paper. Fill the rest of the blender with warm water.

2 Run the blender slowly at first, then at a higher speed, until it creates a smooth substance with no large pieces of paper. If you want, add the flowers or seeds for extra color or texture. This should take about 45 seconds. Stir in any bits of yarn or thread at the end.

3 Now you need to make the mold. Take the brownie pan and cut out the bottom with the scissors, so that it's hollow. Leave about a half-inch border from the edge.

4 Cut the window screening so it's a couple of inches larger on each side than the opening at the bottom of the brownie pan. Place it over the opening and wrap the rubber bands around the sides of the brownie pan to hold it in place.

20

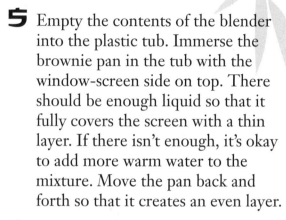

5 Empty the contents of the blender into the plastic tub. Immerse the brownie pan in the tub with the window-screen side on top. There should be enough liquid so that it fully covers the screen with a thin layer. If there isn't enough, it's okay to add more warm water to the mixture. Move the pan back and forth so that it creates an even layer.

6 Take the brownie pan out of the tub. Rub your finger across the surface of the pulp to remove any excess material and water. There should be a flat, uniform layer on top of the screen. You can also press gently with the sponge to remove some of the extra water.

7 Lay the cloth out on a flat surface. Take the brownie pan and CARE-FULLY flip it upside down, letting the pulp fall onto the cloth. Gently remove the pan and screen, leaving behind the pulp.

8 Place a couple of the paper towels on top of the paper pulp. Use the rolling pin to squeeze out any excess moisture. Remove the paper towels. Then let your paper dry overnight. In the morning, your paper should be ready to go!

DID YOU KNOW?

A written record from 93 BCE mentions an interesting story. It says that an imperial guard told a prince that when he had a cold, he should cover his nose with a piece of paper. You might say this was the world's first Kleenex!

WRITING AND EDUCATION

Paper and moveable-type printing were two of the most important inventions to come from ancient China. They made it easier to spread knowledge and education. And getting a good education was the best way to become successful in society. Unless you were lucky enough to be the emperor's son or daughter!

Most education began with ideas from **Confucianism**. But many different things determined what kind of an education someone might pursue. Whether a student lived in the city or the country made a big difference in how they were educated. Whether they were rich or poor was also very important.

There was not just one school system in ancient China. Instead, there were lots of different choices. The empire

tried to provide funding for state academies. This allowed the poorer students to go to school. Think of it as an ancient scholarship!

There were also different ways to become a scholar in ancient China. Teachers were usually older men who had passed the **Chinese Civil Service Exam**. This test was very hard. It asked questions about Confucianism, literature, history, and writing. It even tested a person's morals! The exam made sure that only the smartest people in the whole country became leaders.

科舉

CHINESE CIVIL
SERVICE EXAM

By 1000 BCE, people wrote using **pictograms**, or drawings of words and objects. There were over 80,000 pictograms to learn! Today, only about 3,000 different characters are used. Children started writing some of the easier characters when they were three or four years old. By the time they were eight, children received simple books about the main Confucian ideas. A teacher said the phrases first. Then the young students repeated these sayings over and over again. Sometimes they repeated the phrases all day until they memorized them by heart. Even at a young age, students often had to memorize as many as 20 or 30 new characters a day!

Teenagers studied at a more advanced school. They studied the writings of Confucius, read literature and poetry, and learned about government and the military. Depending on the school, they might have the chance to write and publish their own books, too!

WORDS TO KNOW

Confucianism: a set of ideas created by a man named Confucius, who lived from 551 to 479 BCE.

Chinese Civil Service Exam: a difficult exam that tested knowledge about Confucianism, literature, history, writing, and even morals.

pictogram: a written symbol that represent a word or object.

But writing and publishing books by hand took a lot of time. So the Chinese looked for ways to make writing easier. They began by carving large stone tablets with backwards images and designs. Then they applied ink to the tablets. Pressing paper against the surface of the tablet made a print. But it took a long time to carve stone tablets. By the eighth century CE, the Chinese came up with a technique called **wood-block printing**. It still took a long time to carve characters into wood, but it was easier and quicker than carving stone.

CONFUCIUS

Few people throughout Chinese history and culture have been more influential than the man known as Confucius. He lived from 551 to 479 BCE during the Eastern Zhou period, in a time when there was lots of social unrest in China. He was very disturbed by the state of Chinese society and wished to share ideas he hoped would make the land more peaceful and harmonious.

孔子
CONFUCIUS

Confucius traveled throughout China trying to express these ideas, which covered everything from family life to government, and warfare to education. Confucius thought that people should act humanely and that government should be responsible and good-natured. He looked to the great kings of the past for examples of how a leader should treat his people with compassion. He thought that education was one of the foundations of life and that every person should try to challenge their mind as much as possible. He believed that respect for one's family, especially elders (like parents and grandparents), was essential. He believed a good person must have outstanding morals. Confucius had great admiration for the arts, like music and painting. He encouraged people to stay creative and make artistic pursuits a major part of life.

Later in his life, he returned home and taught until his death. He made sure to teach his students poetry, history, music, and Chinese traditions. Today, Confucian thought is the backbone of Chinese education and many Chinese beliefs and customs.

DID YOU KNOW?

The Civil Service Examination was used in China from the seventh century all the way up to 1911.

Artists, writers, and government officials used wood-block printing. It became one of the most precious art forms in Chinese history. Once the wood was carved, it was easy to make a lot of prints. A good shop could print up to 1,500 pages a day!

But printers had to start from scratch and carve a new block each time they wanted to make a different print. This meant that many books were still copied by hand because it took less time! Then in 1041 CE, a man named Bi Sheng made separate blocks for the most commonly used characters. Now the characters could be taken out and moved around.

This was the birth of **moveable type** and it was a huge improvement. Once a printer had made blocks of all the characters he needed (which still could be several thousand!), he just needed to rearrange them each time he wanted to make a new print. Imagine writing a book. Before the invention of moveable type, you would have to carve out the entire book. But, if you had a collection of all the letters in the alphabet, you would simply pick out the letters and put them in the right order. As printing became more common, the price of books became much cheaper. So families could keep libraries at home for their children to read and study.

WORDS TO KNOW

wood-block printing: a printing process where images are carved into a large piece of wood, which is then inked and pressed onto paper.

moveable type: an important advance in printing where individual characters could be rearranged easily, allowing for books to be printed more cheaply.

MAKE YOUR OWN MOVEABLE TYPE

In this activity, you'll learn how to make your own moveable type of simple Chinese characters (or a cool design of your own) using ordinary household materials.

1 Start out by folding the piece of paper into four equal pieces and cutting them, so you're left with four smaller sheets of paper. Decide which character will be on your stamp. There are many throughout this book to choose from.

SUPPLIES

piece of white paper 8½ by 11 inches

scissors

#2 pencil

red rubber eraser *(or several if you'd like to make a whole set of characters)*

stick with a rounded edge *(a chopstick, popsicle stick, or the end of a pen or pencil should work fine)*

pen with a fine point

sewing needle or Xacto knife *(have your parents help out with this step)*

inkpad

OPTIONAL

small piece of sandpaper or a nail file

Elmer's glue or wood glue

sponge

small piece of wood

DID YOU KNOW?

After the invention of moveable type, the price of books dropped more than 90 percent. Talk about a great sale!

2 Draw the character of your choice onto the paper with your pencil. Don't make it too big. It has to fit with the pencil on the flat side of the eraser. Use the eraser to draw an outline of its shape on the paper to help get a better idea of its size. Also, be sure that you press hard when you draw the character on the paper, so that it is shiny. This will be important for the next step.

3 Next, you will actually copy the image of the character from the paper to the eraser. Here's how. First, lay the eraser on a flat surface and place your character face-down on the eraser.

4 Take the chopstick or end of a pencil and gently rub the back of the paper, so that the lead from the pencil leaves a pattern on the face of the eraser. Be careful to rub evenly and keep the paper still so you don't smudge your design.

5 Lift the paper off the eraser. You should have the outline of your character on the eraser. Don't worry that it's in reverse! It's supposed to look that way. If the design is smudged, or you don't like the way it looks, you should be able to rub off the pencil with your finger or a wet towel and try again with one of the other sheets of paper. If you like the way the design looks, take the pen and carefully trace around the edges of the character, so that you have a solid, visible, and neat outline.

MOVEABLE TYPE

6 Have your parents help out or supervise for this step. First, take the needle and carve the outer edges of your design. This will help make the carving easier. Then, take the Xacto knife and very carefully begin to shave away all of the areas of the eraser that DO NOT have a design on them, so that when you are finished, the character will be raised a little bit off the surface of the eraser. If you have a small piece of sandpaper or a nail file, this is a good time to use it. You can lightly use the sandpaper or file to shave down the surface you carved away, if it's still a little bit rough.

7 If you want to make your stamp more official-looking, cut the sponge with the scissors so that it's roughly the same size as the eraser. Glue the sponge to the back of the rubber eraser (the side that you didn't carve). Then glue the small piece of wood to the sponge.

8 After everything dries, you'll have your first character! Try it out. First, lightly ink your stamp with the inkpad. Then press the character on a blank sheet of paper. Don't worry if it's not perfect. Being a printer in ancient China was a master craft, and it took years of experience and training to perfect the art. You can continue to make other characters or designs and build up a collection. Most printers in ancient China had at least 3,000 different characters that they used!

MAKE YOUR OWN INK

Many people credit a Chinese philosopher named Tien-Lcheu as the inventor of ink. It's believed he came up with the original recipe for what's known as "Indian ink" in the year 2697 BCE. That's almost 5,000 years ago! His recipe used a combination of lamp oil, soot from pine smoke, the gelatin from a donkey's skin, and musk from a deer.

SUPPLIES

½ to 1 cup of ripe berries *(your choice of strawberries, blackberries, raspberries)*

strainer

bowl that you don't mind getting a little ink stained!

spoon

½ teaspoon vinegar

½ teaspoon salt

small paintbrush

paper

glass jar

1 Place a small amount of the berries in the strainer and hold it over the bowl. Use the back of the spoon to crush the berries. Let the juice flow into the bowl, leaving only the pulp in the strainer. Continue adding berries until you've crushed your entire supply.

2 Once you've collected enough juice in your jar, add the vinegar and salt to help preserve the ink.

3 Dip your brush in the ink and practice Chinese calligraphy on the paper. It may take a few tries to get the hang of it. You need the right amount of ink on the brush so that it isn't too drippy but you still have enough to paint with. You can store the ink in a small, tightly sealed jar.

WARRIORS AND WEAPONS

In many ancient societies, warfare was an honorable way of life. But in China, the military was not always well-respected. In fact, an old saying reminded people that "good iron is not used for nails, and good men do not become soldiers." The Chinese have always placed great importance on living a peaceful life, and soldiers often ranked low in society.

But the ancient world was a violent place. As China grew and became richer, threats from the outside increased. China needed a strong army to protect itself. So the military became a bigger part of the government and daily life. A large part of each dynasty's expenses went to the military.

DID YOU KNOW?

An ancient Chinese weapon called a halberd, which was like a combination of a battle axe and a spear, was sharp enough to split a hair in two!

Emperors wanted the strongest armies possible. Luckily, some of the most brilliant minds in the country were military engineers. They invented new weapons that changed the way armies fought. These weapons allowed the Chinese military to win many battles. But they also made warfare more violent. As a result, many more people died.

The most famous Chinese military invention was gunpowder. The first gunpowder experiments took place around 850 CE. Scientists mixed a chemical called saltpeter with sulfur and charcoal to create an explosion. The Chinese used gunpowder for harmless things like fireworks, but also for weapons.

FIREWORKS

For thousands of years, the Chinese have celebrated with fireworks. They even used fireworks before the invention of gunpowder. As early as 200 BCE people threw pieces of bamboo into fires, setting off small explosions. Once gunpowder was invented, people took fireworks to a whole new level. They mixed all kinds of materials in with the gunpowder to create new colors. Steel dust and iron shavings created a sparkling effect. The indigo plant created a bright blue-green flash. And cotton fibers created violet. It's a good thing people in ancient China took so much time to come up with all of these variations. Otherwise our celebrations like New Year's Eve and the Fourth of July would not be the same!

DID YOU KNOW?

One style of crossbow weighed more than 600 pounds. It could shoot seven-foot long arrows over 1,000 yards.

Archaeologists have discovered hand-held flamethrowers and flaming arrows dating from the tenth century. Other weapons soon followed, such as bombs, grenades, mines, and rockets.

Another very important weapon invented by the Chinese was the crossbow. By 200 BCE the crossbow was well developed and widely used throughout China. Crossbows could be pulled much tighter than a regular bow and arrow and were much more accurate. It was such a cherished invention that there was even a law against taking the crossbow outside of China! Chinese armies came to rely on the crossbow for over a thousand years. There was not just one version of the crossbow, but many different models.

冶金
METALLURGY

The Chinese used dozens of other weapons, including the catapult and the **battering ram**. They were also brilliant at **metallurgy**, which is the science of using metals. They made strong iron swords, suits of armor, bronze-

WORDS TO KNOW

battering ram: a huge, heavy log carried by many people. When used with force, it can break down large walls.

metallurgy: the study and understanding of different metals.

cavalry: an army of soldiers on horseback.

stirrup: a metal ring with a flat bottom attached to a leather strap. Stirrups hang from both sides of a saddle on a horse. Riders put their feet in the stirrups to give them greater control.

tipped spears, and bronze axes. Chinese armies even used screens and curtains for protection them from flying missiles! It wasn't enough for the Chinese to create these dangerous weapons. They also invented new methods for making them quickly, inexpensively, and in great quantities.

The Chinese came up with many new ideas themselves. But they also borrowed ideas from other cultures. From nomadic people, such as the Mongols, the Chinese learned how to organize their army into a **cavalry**. A cavalry is an army made up of soldiers on horseback. Cavalries could travel great distances much faster than foot soldiers. But cavalries would not have been possible without two very important innovations: the saddle and the **stirrup**.

騎兵
CAVALRY

THE STIRRUP

馬鐙
STIRRUP

Have you ever ridden a horse? If you have, you know that holding onto a bare horse without stirrups or a saddle is no easy task. But sure enough, for many generations, horseback riders used nothing to support their feet. Many of the greatest armies in the ancient world, such as those in Rome, Egypt, and Greece, had no stirrups at all for their horseman. Riders' feet dangled and they had far less control over their horse. Some historians think the earliest stirrups were used by the nomads of Central Asia, like the Mongols, who spent almost all of their time on horseback. The nomads probably looped a piece of rope for stirrups. In the third century, the Chinese used their metal-making skills to make sturdy, long-lasting stirrups out of bronze or iron. With a pair of stirrups, mounting a horse just like in the movies became a cinch.

KITES

Have you ever flown a kite on the beach or over a large open area? Maybe you've thought about how beautiful and peaceful they are, drifting through the wind. What you probably don't realize is that those same pretty kites were actually invented thousands of years ago as a tool in warfare!

風箏
KITE

China invented kites sometime around the fifth century BCE. The first kites used lightweight Chinese silk for the sail. Stronger silk was used for string. The kite's framework was made out of bamboo. But it was expensive and difficult to build kites mostly out of silk. After several hundreds of years, people began

THE TERRACOTTA ARMY

The most famous army in Chinese history was never even alive. In 1974 a farmer came across an amazing discovery while digging in his field. Archaeologists who dug up the site found more than 7,000 terracotta (baked earthen clay, or ceramic) statues of Chinese soldiers. The army was part of a huge burial site dedicated to the First Emperor of China, ordered to be built by his subjects. His name was Qin Shi Huangdi and he ruled from 221 to 210 BCE.

All of the statues were lifesize. Each one had a different expression on its face modeled after real people. Even their hair and eyes were different. The Terracotta Army looked just like a real army. There were even clay horses and chariots buried! The Emperor believed that he would need a full army to protect him when he entered the afterlife. The Terracotta Army is now one of the great wonders of the ancient world and is a huge tourist site in China today.

THE ART OF WAR

The Chinese created many new weapons, but these were only a part of their military skill. They also invented new ways to organize their armies and fight more effectively on the battlefield. One of the masterpieces of Chinese military strategy is a book called *The Art of War*, written by Sun Tzu in the sixth century BCE. Sun Tzu explains how to understand the enemy, design a successful attack, manage an army's budget, and much more. *The Art of War* is popular even today. The U.S. Army keeps a copy of it in most of its libraries.

知己知彼, 百戰百勝

"If you know both yourself and your enemy, you will come out of one hundred battles with one hundred victories."
From *The Art of War*

using paper instead. This made kites much more popular and available to common people.

Kites had many uses. But their most common use was for military signaling and communications. This was long before armies had walkie-talkies or radios. Instead, soldiers and commanders used kites to communicate with each other from long distances. Kites could even be used to drop gunpowder bombs into walled cities.

(是故) 百戰百勝, 非善之善者也
不戰而屈人之兵, 善之善者也

"Therefore one hundred victories in one hundred battles are not the most skillful. Seizing the enemy without fighting is the most skillful. War is of vital importance to the state and should not be engaged carelessly." From *The Art of War*

MAKE YOUR OWN ANIMATED

It took several hundred thousand workers and craftsmen more than 30 years to make all of the soldiers in the actual Terracotta Army. You might not have that kind of time to spare—but here's a fun activity you can do that the ancient craftsmen wouldn't have been able to—make your own "terracotta animation." To make your animation, you'll need access to a digital camera and computer. Obviously, the real terracotta soldiers were not movable, because they were made of baked earthen clay. But you'll be able to move yours in all kinds of different poses and directions and have them star in your very own short animated film!

SUPPLIES

- box of large, heavy-duty paperclips
- needlenose pliers to bend the paperclips
- small styrofoam ball
- Sculpey clay *(available from any arts and crafts store)*
- Sculpting/modeling tools *(available from an arts and crafts store or use household utensils)*
- computer *(to make a stop-motion movie)*
- digital camera or camcorder *(for the stop-motion movie)*

Maybe you've seen *Wallace & Gromet, Gumby* television episodes or *The Nightmare Before Christmas.* All of these movies, and many more, use a kind of animation called "claymation." Instead of drawing by hand or using computer graphics like *Toy Story* or *Shrek,* claymation is a technique where animators use a small, 3-D model or puppet to make an animation. Each time they move the model, they take a new picture of its pose. If you continue to move the model little by little and take a picture each time, when you put it all together, your brain thinks the model is actually moving on its own. It takes 12 different pictures, or frames, to make one second of animation. That means a 90-minute movie will need 64,800 pictures! Today, China is one of the world's best countries for animation and many artists still use this claymation technique.

TERRACOTTA ARMY

1   We'll start by making an armature. Think of the armature as the skeleton of your terracotta soldier. It's what will let you bend the model and hold its pose in place. Unbend six paper clips so they're straight. Each will be like a different bone. Set aside two clips for the legs, bending the edges of each with the pliers to make little feet.

2   Take out another paper clip to use as the body. Bend it in half, so that both edges are touching. Attach the legs to the body by wrapping the "non-foot" end of each paper clip around the looped side of the torso. Wrap the end piece of each leg around the torso once or twice, so that they hold in place.

3   Use one paper clip for both arms. Place it by the midsection of the torso, then wrap the paper clip around the body to hold it in place.

4   Now you just need to attach the head. If you have a small Styrofoam ball, you can attach it directly to the top of the body. If not, you can crumple up some newspaper into a ball and poke it on the top of the body.

TERRACOTTA ARMY

5 Here's the fun part—making your skeleton look like a terracotta warrior. Go online to get an idea of what the terracotta warriors looked like. Use the clay to build body parts around the armature. Piece by piece, wrap the paper clips with clay, to resemble a terracotta warrior. You might start with one color, like brown or tan, to make all of the major body parts. Be sure that you use enough clay to cover the paper clips but not so much that the clay falls off. Use other colors for the armor, helmet, and facial features.

6 You might want to come up with a short story or script to follow for your movie. If the story requires a second soldier, make another! If you get really ambitious, you can make some scenery or backgrounds for your short movie.

7 Now, you're ready to animate! If you have a Mac, go to http://www.boinx.com/download/ and download a program called "Boinx iStop Motion." You'll be able to use the program for free as a demo, but first you'll need to register. If you have a PC, you can download a free program called "Animator DV Simple" from http://animatordv.com/download7.

8 Be sure you have a digital camera or camcorder connected to your computer. Both programs work almost the same. There's a red record button in the center of the screen. Each time you want to take a new picture, or frame, all you have to do is click the button. Get your soldier in the pose you want, then click the button. Move the soldier just a tiny bit, then take another picture. If you move the model too much, the motion will be jagged. But don't worry—after a couple of tries, you'll get the hang of it!

9 Play around with different ways to move your soldier and different kinds of backgrounds. Soon enough, you'll have your very own "Terracotta Warrior Short Film!" If you keep it up, you might be on your way to Hollywood before you know it!

MAKE AN ACTUAL TERRACOTTA CLAY ARMY

SUPPLIES

- newspaper
- paper clips
- needlenose pliers
- terracotta clay *(available at most arts and crafts stores)*
- carving tools

If you don't have the technology to film a short animation, don't worry! You can still make an authentic-style terracotta warrior.

1 Spread some newspaper out on your work surface before starting, so you don't make a mess. Build a paper-clip armature as described in the previous activity.

2 Be sure that you're going to finish the soldier in one sitting—the clay doesn't need to be baked and will harden just by being out in the open. Go online to get an idea of what the terracotta warriors looked like. But remember, each one of the warriors was unique. There were even some that were not soldiers at all—like farmers and cooks. So be creative and come up with your own personality and pose!

3 Start with the body. You'll want to build up a good, strong base around the torso. All of the other limbs will be attaching directly to it. Build each limb. Be sure to make each limb thick enough that it will stay together and fully cover the armature, but not so heavy that it will fall off the armature.

4 It's okay to build the soldier larger than you want it to be. You can always carve details into the clay, or shave off excess clay to create the designs you want. Add extra details, like hair, shoes, or armor by attaching separate pieces of clay. Sculpture is all about being creative—so be open and try a bunch of different ways. If you mess up you can always just smoosh your model and start over again.

5 Once you're happy, set your model aside in a safe, dry place. Depending on the exact type of clay you used and how thick your model is, it will take about 24 hours for it to dry, or "cure." Let it sit overnight and when you return, you'll have your very own terracotta warrior sculpture ready to display!

MAKE YOUR OWN KITE

SUPPLIES

two thin plant stakes at least 36 inches long, made from bamboo, plastic, or wood *(available at most hardware stores or nurseries)* or wooden sticks of the same length

heavy-duty scissors or a small wood saw *(ask your parents for help with this!)*

spool of string or twine

strong tape and Elmer's wood glue

two small screw eyes

utility knife

large piece of paper *(poster roll paper works great for this)*

pen or pencil

construction or tissue paper

magic markers or paint to decorate the kite

In this activity, you will learn how to build your own functioning kite. But be careful. Don't use it to declare war on any of your neighbors!

1. The main framework of the kite will be made with the two plant stakes. One will be longer than the other, so first you'll need to cut both to the right lengths. There's no set rule for this—but you should try to make the kite large enough so that it will catch enough wind to stay afloat. Depending on how long your sticks are, try cutting the shorter stick to around 30 inches, and the longer one to around 36 to 40 inches.

2. Position the two sticks so they make a cross. Place the shorter stick about one-quarter of the way down from one end of the longer one.

3 Use the string to tie the two sticks together. Wrap the string around the cross in different directions where the two sticks touch and fasten them together. Apply glue to help keep things in place and make the joint strong. Allow time for the glue to dry.

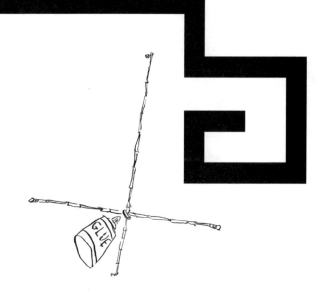

4 Twist the screw eyes into the ends of the top and bottom of the longer stick. Then, use the utility knife to cut small slits in the ends of the shorter stick.

5 Start with one end of the string and wrap it around the bottom screw eye several times, and then tie it. This will be your starting point with the string. Without cutting the string, continue and connect it to the shorter stick by sliding the string through the notch you made. When you get to the second screw eye, wrap it around several times just like you did on the first one. Then, continue to the other short stick, placing the string in its notch. When you get back to the first screw eye, tie off the string, and cut away the excess. The string should now make an outline connecting all of the edges of the sticks and should be pretty tight, but not tight enough to break the sticks.

6 On a table, lay the kite frame on top of the paper. Trace an outline of the string frame on the paper (it should be roughly diamond shaped). When you cut out the paper sail, cut it about 2 inches larger on each side than the shape you traced. This is because you will need to fold over all of the edges once you attach it to the frame.

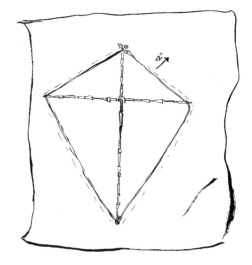

KITE

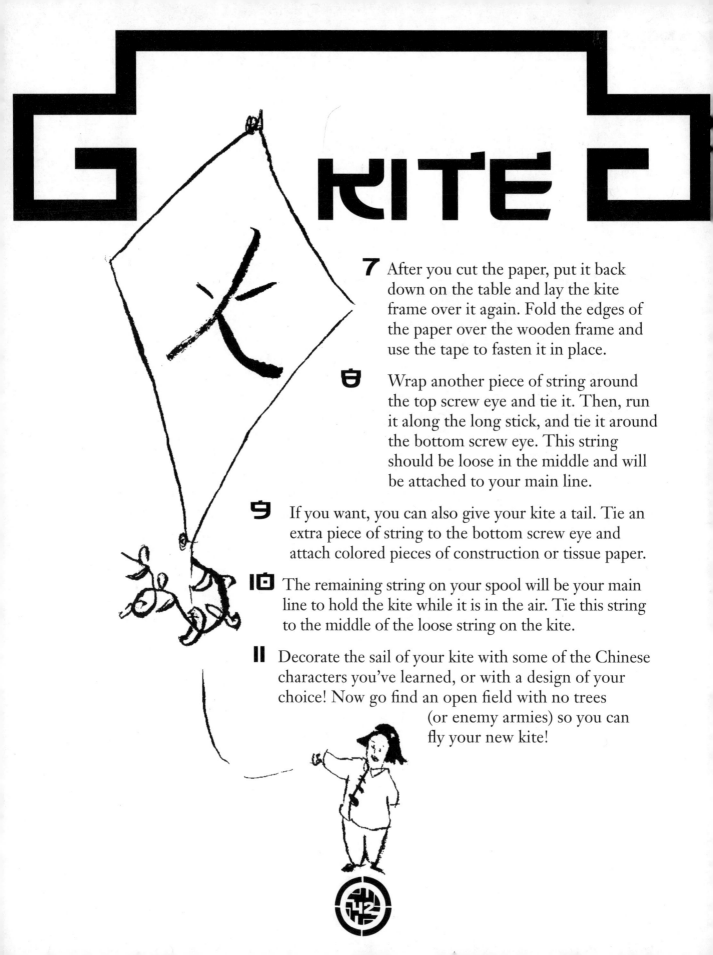

7 After you cut the paper, put it back down on the table and lay the kite frame over it again. Fold the edges of the paper over the wooden frame and use the tape to fasten it in place.

8 Wrap another piece of string around the top screw eye and tie it. Then, run it along the long stick, and tie it around the bottom screw eye. This string should be loose in the middle and will be attached to your main line.

9 If you want, you can also give your kite a tail. Tie an extra piece of string to the bottom screw eye and attach colored pieces of construction or tissue paper.

10 The remaining string on your spool will be your main line to hold the kite while it is in the air. Tie this string to the middle of the loose string on the kite.

11 Decorate the sail of your kite with some of the Chinese characters you've learned, or with a design of your choice! Now go find an open field with no trees (or enemy armies) so you can fly your new kite!

JADE AND SILK

Have you ever been to a museum and looked at objects from ancient China? If so, you've probably seen something carved out of a beautiful, green, almost clear-looking stone. That stone is jade (or *yu* in Chinese). For over 6,000 years, jade has been used in China for jewelry, carvings, sculptures, and even weapons.

The Chinese believed that jade was the most treasured and sacred material in nature. In fact, there are over 500 Chinese characters based on the syllable for "jade." These characters usually have meanings such as beauty, prosperity, or purity. The Chinese thought that jade represented the very best things about humans. It's no wonder the ancient Chinese considered jade to be more valuable than gold or silver!

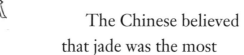

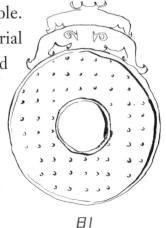

BI

玉

JADE

Jade is a very hard material. It's tough and durable. This means that jade is an extremely difficult material to work with. Imagine trying to carve an intricate and detailed work of art into such a hard stone. But the Chinese were able to do so. No other culture used jade as much as ancient China did. Many of the oldest jade pieces discovered in China are small pieces of jewelry, like necklaces and earrings. The Chinese artists who worked with jade were some of the most talented craftsmen in the ancient world.

At first, jade designs were simple, like the small flat disks with a hollow hole in the middle called *bi*. These looked almost like lime-flavored Lifesavers (but you probably wouldn't want to eat a *bi*). They would often be decorated with golden dragons or other mystical creatures. *Cong* were small hollow jade objects in the shape of a tube. Both were considered great treasures. Only the wealthiest people in the empire owned them.

Later in China's history, during the Zhou and Han dynasties, jade carving became much more complex. Jade artisans created very detailed carvings of flowers, dragons, or other imaginary animals. They even made weapons out of jade!

CONG

WORDS TO KNOW

cocoon: a silky protective case spun by young insects.

loom: a large, frame-like machine that stretches fibers and allows the weaver to stitch, or twist, them together.

prism: a clear triangular-shaped object that can reflect the full color range of the rainbow.

JADE BURIAL SUITS

Just like the pharaohs in ancient Egypt, some wealthy Chinese believed it was important to preserve the body for the afterlife. They thought that jade had special powers to keep the body fresh. Archaeologists have found several ancient burial suits that are made entirely of thousands of pieces of jade! The jade pieces were fastened with very thin strands of gold wire. Imagine being wrapped up in two thousand stones!

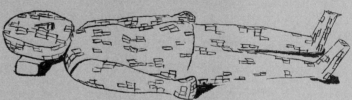

SILK

Right after jade, the next most-prized material in ancient China was silk. This was a big business. Silk is one of the strongest natural fibers in the world. In ancient China, silk was used for many different things, such as dresses, robes, tapestries, and all kinds of artistic decorations. Archaeologists date the origins of silk back to 3000 BCE, and possibly as far back as 6000 BCE.

SILKWORM ON MULBERRY LEAF

The process for creating silk is an old, strange, and delicate one that took many years to perfect. Special kinds of worms, called silkworms, naturally produce silk for their **cocoons**. Silk weavers raised these silkworms in their homes. This gave them greater control over the worms and meant they didn't have to go out into the wild to find them. Often women and children were the ones who raised the silkworms.

A cocoon is a shell that young insects make for themselves for protection as they grow up. It takes six weeks from birth until silkworms start spinning their cocoons. During that time, the silkworms need regular feeding, nurturing, and round-the-clock attention. They mostly eat leaves from the mulberry tree. The slightest neglect means their silk will be unsatisfactory.

Once the silkworm is ready to spin its cocoon, it's moved onto a large tray or flat surface where it has plenty of space to move around. The silkworm starts to spin silk yarn around itself very tightly. This becomes the cocoon. If you were to unwind the thread from one cocoon, it could measure as long as 3,000 feet!

Once the silk fibers were collected from the cocoons, they were taken to a weaver in the city. Weavers rolled the fibers together by hand, which was very hard work. Luckily, **looms** were invented. These large, frame-like machines stretched the fibers and allowed the weaver to stitch, or twist, them together. Some looms were as big as an entire room. The biggest workshops had as many as a dozen looms, all working at the same time.

織布機
LOOM

When the silk fibers were woven together, they created a beautiful, shiny, and elegant fabric. Silk fabrics were prized and desired in China and throughout the ancient world. They were also expensive, because of the time and expertise required to make silk. Silk weavers and traders kept the process for making silk a big secret. Only a few people knew how to make it.

DID YOU KNOW?

Silk fibers shimmer because they contain microscopic structures that are prism-shaped. Prisms reflect all different colors of light in bright and vibrant ways.

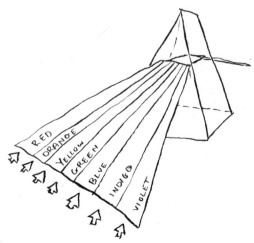

MAKE YOUR OWN JADE BI JEWELRY

SUPPLIES

- paper plate
- green and yellow Sculpey clay
- clay modeling tool or plastic utensil
- toothpick
- index card
- oven
- tin foil pan or tray
- elastic thread or string
- scissors

Actual jade might be very expensive and hard to find, but you can still make your own replica of an ancient Chinese *bi*! Jade artisans made pieces in all different forms. So use your imagination and make other shapes or designs out of your "Sculpey jade" too!

1 Use the paper plate as your work surface. Right out of the package the Sculpey clay might still be very hard to mold. Loosen and warm it by working it back and forth in your hands. Break off a small piece of green clay and roll it into a worm shape about a half-inch thick. Connect the ends together so that it forms a ring. Slightly flatten the ring, so it looks like a Lifesaver.

2 Traditional *bi* pendants often had a dragon crawling around the ring. Create a small dragon out of yellow Sculpey clay. Attach it to the ring so that it wraps around it and won't fall off. You might also want to inscribe a name or word onto the surface of the *bi* ring. Use your modeling tool or toothpick to do this.

3 Place your jade ring on the index card to keep it from sticking to the pan. Then place the *bi* and index card in the foil pan. Follow the baking directions on the packaging of your clay. Usually Sculpey clays need to bake at 275 degrees Fahrenheit for about 15 minutes. Be careful—the clay won't fully harden until it's completely cool.

4 Once your *bi* is cool and hard, measure out a necklace from the thread that will be the right size to fit over your head. You'll want the *bi* to hang right around the middle of your chest. Cut the piece of thread, leaving a little extra room for tying the ends together. Pull the thread through the *bi* ring. To be sure that your *bi* won't fall off, wrap the thread around the *bi* a couple of times right in the middle of the string. Once your thread is secure, tie the ends together.

MERCHANTS AND TRADE

Walking through a marketplace in seventh-century China was an amazing experience. A shopper might find spices, **indigo**, ivory, and silver from thousands of miles away. The Chinese made wonderful things too, and many of their products were regarded as exotic treasures across the world.

Throughout the East Indies, Europe, and Africa, merchants sold Chinese jade, pottery, rice wine, silk, and **porcelain**. But, without planes, trains, and automobiles, how was all of this possible? Merchants usually traveled by land in wagons. But sometimes it was difficult, especially in northern China.

Ships could only sail down rivers in the north for short distances. And travel by horse-drawn wagons took a long time. It was also very expensive.

On the other hand, there were several rivers in southern China that were much easier to navigate. In particular, the Yangzi River could be traveled on by ship for over 1,500 miles. Merchants could also sail down the many smaller rivers shooting off from the Yangzi. So it wasn't that hard to reach many different ports across southern China. All it took was a smart and somewhat adventurous merchant.

瓷

PORCELAIN

The Chinese never let mountains stand in the way of trade or travel. North and South China stayed divided for a long time because there was no easy way to travel between the two regions. But the empires eventually built a series of roads and canals for trade and communication. This was also part of an effort to make China a more unified country.

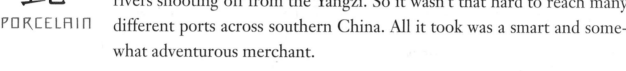

SUSPENSION BRIDGES

If you've ever driven across a river in a big city, chances are you've crossed over a suspension bridge. Suspension bridges are amazing feats of engineering. They can support thousands of cars and trucks each day. Of course, bridges in ancient China didn't need to worry about supporting cars and trucks, but they used the same basic design as bridges today.

Bridges made from wood, steel, or iron rest right on top of supports. A suspension bridge, on the other hand, uses ropes or cables to hold it up. This means that it can extend for very long distances without supports.

In ancient China, suspension cables were first made from bamboo and later with iron chains. Wooden planks were laid close together to make a pathway to walk across. Chinese bridges were incredibly sturdy—but it still took some guts to walk across them!

The first emperor, Qin Shi Huangdi (221–210 BCE), built one of China's most important roads. It was 4,350 miles long and connected the capital city to the most distant parts of the empire. By the end of the second century CE, China already had more than 22,000 miles of roads!

The ancient Chinese also built many bridges. Most of the bridges they built used a beam design. This meant their basic structure was a wooden or stone beam. They also built arch bridges as well as the world's first suspension bridges.

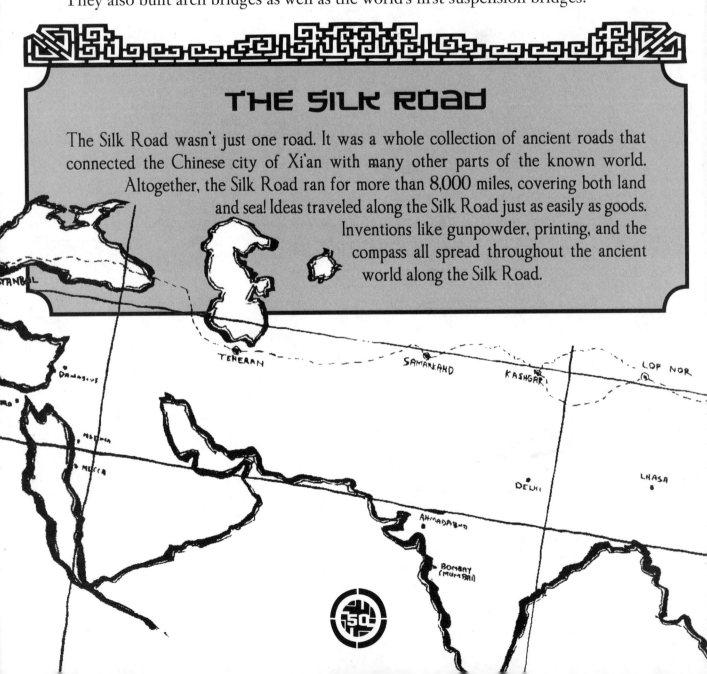

THE SILK ROAD

The Silk Road wasn't just one road. It was a whole collection of ancient roads that connected the Chinese city of Xi'an with many other parts of the known world. Altogether, the Silk Road ran for more than 8,000 miles, covering both land and sea! Ideas traveled along the Silk Road just as easily as goods. Inventions like gunpowder, printing, and the compass all spread throughout the ancient world along the Silk Road.

But travel along China's many roads was slow. It was also difficult and expensive to maintain thousands of miles of roads. Travel by water was faster and cheaper. So the Chinese built canals. Rivers in China generally run west to east, dividing the country into north-south regions. Canals were a brilliant way to connect the two regions and unify the country. The first big canal ever built in the world was in China. It's known as "The Magic Canal" and is still in use today, 2,200 years later!

During the seventh century, the Chinese started building the Grand Canal, the longest ancient canal in the world. It helped bring together five large water systems. Altogether the Grand Canal stretched for over

DID YOU KNOW?

Archaeologists have discovered wheels in China that date from around 1500 BCE.

1,100 miles. It became even easier to travel on the Grand Canal after gate locks were invented in the tenth century. These were special sections throughout the canal to help raise or lower boats from one level of water to another.

鎖

GATE LOCKS

Trade could not just happen anywhere. The government was very strict about where merchants could sell their goods. It set up special official marketplaces and decided when they could be open for business. Government officials also kept a close watch on the quality of goods and workmanship. A merchant who sold goods of bad quality would not stay in business very long!

One thing that made China special was its desire to standardize trade. This meant making things the same for everybody. The Chinese did this in two ways: through weights and measures, and coinage.

DID YOU KNOW?

Chang Heng invented the world's first seismograph, which is an instrument used for recording earthquakes. You'll learn more about Chang Heng's seismograph on page 104.

Archaeologists have discovered bronze coins dating from as early as the fifth century BCE. By the eleventh century CE, Chinese coins were used throughout Asia. The Qin Emperor was one of the first to start a one-coin currency for the entire country. It was a round copper coin with a square hole in the middle.

Chinese mints, or factories that produce coins, certainly stayed very busy. Some historians believe that they produced as many as 6 billion coins per year! Eventually, the Chinese saw that bronze coins were too heavy for long-distance trade and travel. They began using paper money to solve this problem.

Today, we know exactly what one pound weighs, or how long a foot is. But for thousands of years, people used body parts to measure things. A foot was the actual length of a person's foot. Of course, every person's body is different, so measurements were not exact.

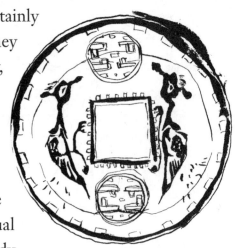

ANCIENT CHINESE COIN
WITH A SQUARE HOLE

THE FOUR DIRECTIONS

Most maps we use today have north on the top and south on the bottom. But ancient Chinese maps were usually the reverse—south was on top and north was on the bottom. South was placed on top because it was believed to be connected with summer and the sun. North was below because it represented winter and water. Also, Chinese maps usually had nine different directions in total—north, northeast, northwest, south, southeast, southwest, west, east and the center.

CARTOGRAPHY

A man named Chang Heng, who lived almost 2,000 years ago, was the father of **cartography**. Cartography is the science of making maps. Of course, people had been making maps for thousands of years before Chang Heng. But he was the first to use **grids** and **coordinates**. This allowed distances and directions to be calculated far more accurately today. Talk about a revolutionary thinker!

It's hard to imagine how important a good map was back in ancient times. But an accurate map could be a military's best secret weapon or a merchant's most powerful tool for trading. Of course, it was also the best way to make sure you never got lost!

WORDS TO KNOW

cartography: the science of making maps.

grid: a series of evenly spaced horizontal and vertical lines.

coordinate: numbers that are used to determine the position of a point.

As China grew bigger, its rulers saw that trade could only prosper with more exact ways to measure things. The Han Dynasty was the first to come up with a whole system of weights and measurements. And they thought of everything. For example, they made sure that all roads had the same width. They also made sure that all carts were the same size. This way, the ruts on every road were the same width and any cart could travel on any road! And because weights were also the same, merchants would not get cheated when they went from one town to another. A pound of rice was the same everywhere.

MAKE YOUR OWN SUSPENSION BRIDGE

SUPPLIES

- box of straws
- scissors
- ruler
- bamboo skewers
- duct tape
- thread, string, or dental floss
- small paper cup
- paper clips
- pennies or dimes

Here's your chance to make your own working model of a suspension bridge. This activity will help you understand the concepts behind the technology Chinese engineers used thousands of years ago. You'll also compare a simple beam bridge to the far stronger suspension bridge.

1　First, you'll need to make the towers for your bridge. These will be the main supports that help hold your suspension cables in place. Cut four pieces of straws down to about 4 inches long each. Cut four bamboo skewers to the same length as the straws. Insert the skewers into the straws. Use a small piece of duct tape at each end of the straw to seal the skewer inside.

2　Take two of the straw/bamboo supports. Using duct tape cut into thin strands, attach the straws together at one end, about ½ centimeter from the edge. Do the same for the other pair of straw/bamboo supports.

3　Now you'll need to make the main span for the bridge. Use a full-length straw and place a bamboo skewer inside. If the skewer is too long, cut it down to size. Seal the edges with duct tape.

4　You'll need to use two tables to test your bridge. Separate the tables so they're just about as far apart as your bridge span. On the edge of each table, use the duct tape to attach the loose ends of the towers. Spread the loose ends about an inch apart from each other.

5　Stick the bridge span between the open ends of each tower. It should be resting freely on the surface edge of each table.

6 In this step you'll turn your project into a full-fledged suspension bridge. Cut a piece of dental floss or string about two feet long. Wrap the middle of the string around the bridge span straw several times. Make sure that the string is centered around the middle of the span.

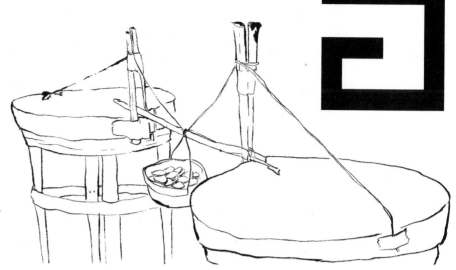

7 Take each loose end of the string and feed it up and over each tower, so that it fits in the space on top, right above the duct tape. Let the string extend as far as it can past the the tower on each side. Tie each end of the string to a paper clip.

8 Use the duct tape to attach the paper clips to each table. But here's the trick: you need to set up the paperclips at the right length from the bridge span so that they create enough tension to support it. The thread should be tight enough that it pulls on the bridge span from both sides. This is what will keep the bridge strong. Also, the paper clips on each side must be exactly the same length apart from the towers. If the string is drooping, pull the paper clips farther away from the towers to make it tighter. But don't pull so tight that you snap your bridge span!

9 By now, your bridge should be tight, strong and ready to travel on! You can test your bridge to see how strong it actually is. Unbend a paper clip so that it has a hook on each end. Drape one end of the paper clip over the middle of the bridgespan. Puncture a hole through the top of a paper cup with the other end of the paper clip, so the cup hangs freely on the paper clip.

10 See how many coins your bridge can hold before it falls. Hopefully, it can hold a lot of change! Keep on loading it up. If it collapses, try to pay attention to where the bridge fails and see if there are ways to strengthen it. If you want to compare how much stronger a suspension bridge is than a regular unsupported span—try testing the span without the string attached. It should collapse pretty easily!

MAKE YOUR OWN RELIEF

Today, most maps we have are two-dimensional, or flat. We have to use our imagination to understand the actual **topography** of the land. The Chinese were the first to create relief maps. These are three-dimensional maps that show people exactly how the land and mountains looked, like miniature models of the landscape. The Chinese made relief maps as early as the third century BCE. Relief maps were extremely helpful for navigation, because explorers and merchants could see the exact **contours**, or shapes, of the **terrain**.

SUPPLIES

access to the Internet or a print atlas

a pencil

2-by-2 foot piece of plywood or poster board *(or an equally hard surface)*

block of sculptor's clay or Sculpey green for land, blue for water

WORDS TO KNOW

topography: the natural features of the land, especially as they appear on a map.

contour: the shape or structure of something.

terrain: an area of land and its natural features (hilly, swampy, dry).

There were many different kinds of relief maps. Some were carved out of rock and others were made out of wood. In some of the emperors' tombs, archaeologists discovered relief maps using the shiny, silver mercury to represent flowing rivers. But remember that mercury is also poisonous! Because of this, many of the most sacred and beautiful tombs in China cannot be explored by archaeologists.

MAP

1. Decide what your relief map will show. It could be a place as large as China. Or you could even create a map of your own neighborhood.

2. Use an atlas to find a map showing elevation (the height of the land), or go online to find a map. Get your parents's permission first. Try maps.google.com, or NASA's topographical map of the United States, which can be found at http://photojournal.jpl.nasa.gov/catalog/PIA03377. Print out your map and use it as a reference.

3. With the pencil, draw an outline of the land onto the plywood or poster board. Try to keep everything to scale. Be sure to mark any rivers, lakes, or oceans.

4. Now take the green clay and use it to fill in the land on the space you outlined. The clay should stick directly to the surface. To start, make a thin, even, flat layer. But make sure not to put clay where rivers or water should be.

5. Look at the map from the atlas or the Internet. In particular, look for hills and mountains. Take more clay and carefully add more to the areas that have higher elevations on the map. Try to make the contour of your own map match the contour of the official map. Use your thumbs and fingers to make the surface of the land on your map feel more rugged. This obviously won't be exact—but you can still try!

地勢
TOPOGRAPHY

6. If you're mapping an area that has water, use the blue clay to fill in the water. Now you have a full relief map that will give you a rough idea of what the land looks like. Take a good look at it. It might even help you prepare for your next big adventure!

EXPLORERS AND SAILING

You've probably learned about famous explorers, such as Christopher Columbus or Ferdinand Magellan. These men sailed across the ocean and discovered parts of the New World. But did you know that Chinese explorers had been sailing a thousand years before Christopher Columbus was even born? And that their ships were much better than the ones used in Europe many years later? In fact, the ancient Chinese were among the most brilliant and fearless sailors and explorers in history!

You might not be old enough to drive a car yet, but you know that steering would be pretty difficult without a steering wheel! Well, for hundreds of years, European ships didn't have a steering wheel. Instead, they used giant oars.

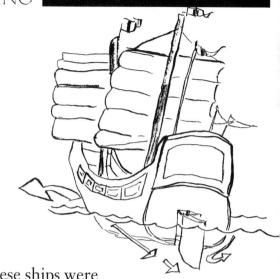

DID YOU KNOW?

The rudder was attached to the stern of the ship with a system of ropes. In this way the rudder could be raised in case the ship traveled through shallow waters. This helped save the rudder from dragging across the ocean floor and getting damaged.

Even though they could be hundreds of feet long, these ships were steered the same way you'd steer a small raft or canoe. Steering oars worked fine for short trips. But it made long-distance travel nearly impossible.

The Chinese were far more inventive. They used **rudders** to steer their boats. A rudder looked like a tail fin on the back of a ship, and it controlled a ship's direction much better than an entire crew of strong rowers. The oldest known image of a rudder in ancient China was from the first century CE.

In 1958 archeologists discovered a two-foot-long clay pottery model of an ancient Chinese **junk** in a tomb near Guangzhou, in Southern China. A junk is not something worthless that you might throw away. Actually, a junk is a style of sailboat that was very popular in ancient China and is still used today. The junk was first developed during the Han Dynasty, between 220 BCE and 200 CE. Unlike other sailboats, a junk has a flat bottom. Also, the **stern**, or back of the boat, was much higher than the **bow**, or front.

On junks, the rudder worked by changing the flow of water past the **hull**, or body, of the ship. Depending on which direction the rudder was pointed, it would cause the boat to turn, or **yaw**,

WORDS TO KNOW

rudder: a piece of wood attached to the back of a ship used for steering.

junk: a style of flat-bottomed sailboat that was very popular in ancient China.

stern: the back of a ship.

bow: the front of a ship.

hull: the main body of a ship.

yaw: the act of turning a ship.

船尾
STERN

in the direction that the ship's captain intended. The rudder itself was made of wood and shaped like a fin.

Perhaps the most important part of a sailboat is the sail. Many sailboats today have sails shaped like triangles. But junks had sails that were more of a square shape. European sails were usually made from large pieces of canvas. The canvas sails caught the wind well, but were clumsy and often hard to control. When a ship with canvas sails changed direction, it took several men to actually climb up and open the sail. Instead, the Chinese used **matting**, a rough material made from natural fibers like grass, for their sails.

The Chinese were also the first to use **battens**. Battens are wooden poles that divide the sail's matting into several smaller sections. They help the sail to be raised and lowered much like horizontal blinds. Battens also let a captain decide how much of the sail he wants to use. For example, he can decide to only raise the sail two battens high. If he wants to travel especially fast, he can go full steam ahead with the entire sail raised. A sail with battens can still be used even if it gets holes in it. If you get holes in a canvas sail, you're flat out of luck!

Chinese ships could also receive heavy damage from an accident or battle and still sail. How on earth could they do this? They were so strong because they had **bulkheads**. A bulkhead is a partition, or section, inside of a ship.

WORDS TO KNOW

matting: a rough material made from natural fibers like grass. This was used for sails.

batten: wooden poles that divide the sail into smaller sections.

bulkhead: a large partition or section inside of a ship. These were often watertight.

ZHENG HE, THE GREAT CHINESE EXPLORER

It would have been almost impossible to find someone in ancient China who traveled more than a man named Zheng He. When he was 34 years old, Zheng He embarked on one of the greatest adventures in the ancient world. From 1405 to 1433 CE, he traveled to almost every place in the known world.

The Ming government helped pay for his trips. The Emperor wanted to spread word of the Chinese empire across the globe. He also thought that Zheng He might help the Ming Dynasty control many of the popular and valuable trade routes.

Zheng He visited Asia, India, the Persian Gulf, Arabia, Africa, and the Americas. Historians estimate that there were at least 27,000 men in Zheng He's crew. This huge group of people included explorers, doctors, and soldiers. And they sailed in a group of 62 ships, some of which are believed to have been over 600 feet long! The Niña, the Pinta, and the Santa Maria (the ships Columbus used to sail to the New World) were only 50 feet long. Compared to them, Zheng He's ships were gigantic.

Think of a bulkhead as a little room. These rooms were actually watertight compartments. There may have been as many as 15 or 20 watertight compartments in the hull of a ship. If the ship was hit and damaged, water might spill into one of these rooms and fill it up. But the ship could still sail because the others stayed closed off and dry. Chinese shipbuilders made sailboats with bulkheads and watertight compartments as early as the second century CE.

All of these innovations would have been meaningless if sailors didn't know where to go. That's why the most important invention for traveling was the compass. You probably know about the North and South Poles. What you may not know is that the earth is actually like a big magnet. The two poles are the most magnetic. The Chinese understood this and began experimenting with a magnetic needle around 100 CE. But it was not until the Song Dynasty, around 1040 CE, that the first magnetic direction finder, or compass, was invented.

The magnetism of each pole always stays the same, no matter where you are. Using a compass, a person always knows which way is north, south, east, and west. Navigation on the open seas would be much harder without a compass.

船
BOAT

The first compass in ancient China was very different from the kind of compass used today. It was called a "wet compass." A small, iron fish was magnetized and placed in a bowl of water. It would always "swim" toward the South Pole. That was one smart fish! The wet compass was often used by the military as a way for soldiers to find their way during the night, when the light and familiar landmarks could not guide them. A later design was called the "hanging compass." Instead of using a bowl of water, a small magnetic turtle was hung by a string from a wooden frame. Sure enough, the turtle's tail always pointed north.

MAKE YOUR OWN COMPASS

SUPPLIES

small magnet

sewing needle or small nail

sewing thread or thin string

pencil or pen

plastic cup

In this activity, you will learn how to make your own ancient Chinese hanging compass. You just might be surprised at how easy it is to create!

1 First magnetize your needle. Take the magnet and rub it along the surface of the needle or nail in one direction. Repeat this at least 30 or 40 times. Be careful not to cut yourself.

2 Cut the string so that it is long enough to hang from the pencil but won't touch the bottom of the cup. Tie one end of the sewing thread or string to the middle of the needle. Try to attach it at a point where it is balanced. Tie the other end of the string to the pen or pencil at its center.

3 Place the pen on top of the plastic cup and let the string hang down. The needle should hang freely about an inch from the bottom of the cup. Slide the string left or right on the needle to help it balance if it tilts too much one way or another.

4 Place your compass on a flat surface. See which direction the needle points. The thicker end of the needle should point north. Now move the compass to a different room. The needle should still point in the same direction. If it does, then mark north on your cup with a pen or magic marker. If it doesn't point in the same direction both times, you might need to re-magnetize it. Just get out the magnet and start rubbing again! If you have a real compass, test it out to see how accurate your hanging needle compass actually is!

MAKE YOUR OWN
ANCIENT

It might take you a lifetime to make a full-sized Chinese junk fit for sailing on the high seas, but it should only take you about 15 minutes to make a miniature one!

1 It's easy to draw the outline of your sail on a piece of paper. Make a 2-inch square in the upper lefthand corner of the paper. Use the ruler to lightly draw a line connecting the bottom right corner of the square to the bottom right corner of the page. Also connect the bottom right corner of the square to the bottom left corner of the page.

2 Cut out your sail from the triangle shape you've just drawn. You should have a slightly lopsided, triangular-looking piece of paper.

3 Take the BBQ skewer and poke it through the top corner of the sail. This will be your mast. Line it up with the bottom of the sail and poke it through the bottom too. Align the skewer so it's perpendicular with the ground. This means that there will be some excess sail hanging over one edge. Don't align the skewer along the edge of the sail.

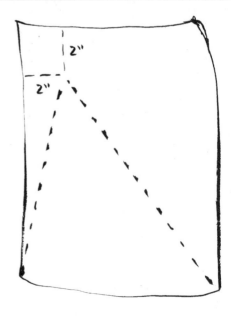

CHINESE JUNK

4 Now you'll attach your battens to the sail. For this size sail, you'll use three battens of different sizes. The first, longest one will go closest to the bottom of the sail. Cut one of the wooden coffee stirrers to about 8 inches in length. Using the tape or glue gun, attach one end to the mast and the other to the bottom corner of the sail.

5 Cut a second coffee stirrer to about 5 inches in length. Attach this batten in the same fashion as the last one, but position it about midway between the top and bottom of the sail.

6 Cut a third coffee stirrer to about 2 inches in length. Attach this one the same way, but up towards the top of the sail. Run a piece of Scotch tape along each batten, so that the entire batten is attached to the sail.

7 Take a glob of Sculpey clay and place it in the bottom of your Tupperware container. Poke the bottom of your mast into the Sculpey clay. Be sure there's enough clay to hold your mast in place. If it's wiggling around too much, add more clay to stabilize it.

8 Fill up your sink or bathtub and set sail with your junk! Try blowing on the sail or use a portable fan to see how it holds up!

HEALERS AND MEDICINE

Few things were more important to the Chinese than a healthy body and mind. From the beggar in the street to the emperor himself, everyone knew that good health was the key to a long and prosperous life.

Ideas about the body and mind almost always began with the *qi*. *Qi* (pronounced "chee") could mean many different things. Usually it represented sensations in the body—touch, heat, cold, pleasure, passion, and pain.

氣
QI

We can't see or hear *qi*. But people understood that this force flowed through the body and was one of the most important parts of life. Imagine a highway in a busy city. When there are no problems, thousands of people can travel in their cars and get where they need to go. But accidents can cause big problems.

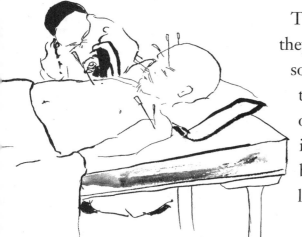

Think about how upset your parents get when they're stuck in traffic! The same rules apply to a person's *qi*. For someone who is healthy and vibrant, their *qi* would move freely, like cars traveling fast on the highway. But for someone who was ill or injured, it was believed that something might be blocking their *qi*, like a traffic jam. And this could lead to sickness, mental illness, or even death.

Most ideas about health in ancient China had to do with making sure the *qi* could flow properly through the body. One of the most famous early medical thinkers was the Yellow Emperor. *The Yellow Emperor's Inner Cannon* is a classic book written sometime around 305–204 BCE. It divided the body into 12 different ***jingmai***. These were channels, or highways, through the body. The *qi* was believed to move through each channel in a certain pattern. The *Inner Cannon* also said that at special points on the body, these channels connected the skin to the body's internal organs. It was at these points that someone with proper training could reach the *qi*. This is the main idea behind **acupuncture**.

You may have heard of acupuncture before. You might think that sticking needles in someone's skin sounds scary or painful. But acupuncture has been practiced in China for over one thousand years.

針刺
ACUPUNCTURE

WORDS TO KNOW

qi: an invisible energy force that flows throughout the entire universe.

jingmai: channels, or highways, that run through the body. The *qi* was believed to move through each channel in a certain pattern.

acupuncture: a form of healing that involves sticking needles into certain points on the body to restore the proper flow of *qi*.

ginseng: a plant grown in China that has many different health benefits.

moxibustion: a form of healing that involves burning an herb right above specific energy points on the body.

GINSENG

Ginseng is a perennial plant (meaning it lives for two or more years) that has been grown in Asia for over a thousand years. It has many different health benefits. Today, ginseng is taken by people in the West as well. The word ginseng comes from the Cantonese word "jan seng," which literally means "man root." This is because the plant was believed to look like a man's legs. People in ancient China valued ginseng very much, because it could treat lots of different health problems. Talk about a useful plant!

人參
GINSENG

Believe it or not, it doesn't actually hurt that much! It's become a popular form of treatment outside of China, too.

Healers in ancient China also used something called **moxibustion**. This is when the healer burned a special herb called mugwort right above the special points on a patient's body. Moxibustion was supposed to help the patient's *qi* flow better. Sometimes, a healer would even burn the mugwort directly onto a person's skin. Obviously, moxibustion and acupuncture weren't for everyone!

We usually only take medicine when we're sick. But in ancient China, people believed you could avoid getting sick in the first place if you kept your mind, body, and spirit strong. In many ways, the Chinese cared for their bodies like a garden. To grow healthy plants, it takes the right amount of food, sunlight, and soil every day. The ancient Chinese thought the body needed to be cared for in the same way.

DID YOU KNOW?

There were also "death points" on the body. A single blow to these could inflict severe pain or even death. They were heavily guarded secrets. In the wrong hands, a murderer could get away with killing someone without leaving behind a single trace.

DID YOU KNOW?

A person trained in acupuncture can help the flow of *qi* in many ways. In addition to using **zhen** (needles), he or she might also apply heated **shi** (stones) to the specific points on the body. These points were called **ashi**, which actually means "oh yes!" because people might yell since it felt so good to get rid of their tension and pain.

This included everything from always eating properly and exercising to practicing one of the many different forms of martial arts.

The Chinese were one of the first people to have a deep knowledge of medicines found in nature. They studied hundreds of plants, herbs, and insects, discovering that many of them can heal and protect the body. The Chinese found brilliant uses for materials that came from their everyday lives. They even found medical uses for human and animal waste! One mythical figure named Shennong is said to have tasted hundreds of different herbs. He then told farmers which plants were safe or poisonous.

Usually a doctor would mix anywhere from two to a dozen different plants and herbs. He would create a blend that was specially made for each patient's body and illness. No two prescriptions were the same! Chinese medicines and herbs were organized in many different ways. They could be organized based on taste or the organ that they treated. Sometimes they were even organized based on how the herb affected the patient's balance of **yin and yang**.

陰楊

YIN AND YANG

Yin and yang was based on the idea that the world is made up of opposites that are also perfectly balanced with each other. The human body also needed to be balanced in this way. For example, the inside of the body needs just as much attention as the outside. And things like heat need to be balanced out with cold.

DID YOU KNOW?

Doctors thought the body worked just like a government. Every organ was like a different government office and together they all worked to form a strong and vibrant empire. Try to imagine what government office each one of your body parts might have been!

Healers were different than doctors. They believed that supernatural powers could cure illness. Supernatural means things that cannot necessarily be proven by math, science, and technology—things like magic or the spiritual world. Spiritual healers were often women. They would use **divination** when trying to heal others, relying on superstition and omens to help figure out a patient's illness. Superstitions are beliefs that deal with things like good luck and bad luck. For example, Chinese superstition said

卜筮
DIVINATION

WORDS TO KNOW

zhen: acupuncture needles.

shi: heated stones that are sometimes used in place of acupuncture needles.

ashi: points where acupuncture needles affect the flow of *qi*.

yin and yang: a belief that the world is balanced by opposing forces.

divination: the use of superstition and omens by healers to help diagnose a patient's illness and predict future recovery.

that cutting your nails at night is a bad idea, because it attracts wandering spirits. An omen is a sign of something to come in the future, either good or bad. For example, seeing a white deer or being offered jade or gold was thought to be a sign of something good to come. Healers could also predict their patient's future recovery. Instead of using herbal medicines, a healer might use the power of the gods, spirits, or ancestors to make people healthy again. Many people also believed that all things on earth—streams, trees, plants, and animals—had a spirit.

LEARN T'ai Ch'i MOVES

You've probably seen kung-fu before. It is fast, exciting, and can be extremely dangerous. This is one reason why kung-fu is in so many Hollywood action movies! But many people don't realize that in China, t'ai ch'i is actually the most commonly practiced form of martial arts, especially for elderly people. T'ai ch'i uses many of the same movements as kung-fu, but its pace and speed are much slower.

T'ai ch'i is about more than just fighting an enemy. It focuses on how a person breathes, stretches, and moves rhythmically. It is very peaceful and relaxing for those who practice it. If you are ever able to go to China, you might see dozens of people practicing t'ai ch'i very early in the morning in the parks. It is quite a sight. Just make sure not to disturb them! But if you're polite and ask to join in, they will probably teach you a few moves.

Until then, you don't need to go all the way to China to learn a little t'ai ch'i. You can learn a few simple t'ai ch'i moves on your own. Go ahead and teach them to friends and start your very own t'ai ch'i group in a park close to where you live!

FARMING

Ancient China had giant cities, but it was mostly a **rural**, agricultural society. This means that most people lived in the countryside and farmed. Because farming was so important back then (and continues to be today), the Chinese used great creativity in discovering new and easier ways to farm.

Many of the farming techniques the Chinese practiced were used thousands of years before the same methods were used in Europe and the West. Thanks to inventions like the ax and the saw, it became easier for the Chinese to clear land and turn swamps and forests into farmland.

The oldest farms in ancient China were on the North China Plain, near the Yellow River. The Yangshao people settled by the banks of the Yellow River around 5000 to 3000 BCE.

淤
SILT

Every spring, the river would flood and leave behind a layer of dirt, or **silt**, which is full of nutrients. This made the soil perfect for growing a great variety of crops, such as rice, barley, wheat, and millet. The Chinese used **irrigation** to help the water reach places farther away from the river.

灌溉
IRRIGATION

The area around the Yangzi River was also very good for farming. The Longshan people lived here around 3000 BCE. They might have eaten rice that grew naturally. The Longshan were more advanced than the Yangshao and raised different kinds of livestock. They also used baked bricks to build stronger homes and were one of the first people in ancient China to build walls around their towns for protection.

Farmers had to use their land wisely. Some crops only grew well during one season, so farmers used a system called "double-cropping." First, farmers created a detailed and exact planting calendar for the year. For example, they would grow rice seedlings in seed beds away from the main farming field during the winter. Archaeologists have found evidence that rice was cultivated as early as 7000 BCE in ancient China. Then in the spring they would carefully switch the grown seedlings into the **paddy fields**. During the summer, farmers weeded and fertilized their precious rice crops.

WORDS TO KNOW

rural: areas in the countryside.

silt: fine-grained soil rich in nutrients, often found at the bottom of rivers or lakes.

irrigation: technique of transporting water through canals to water crops.

domesticate: to raise animals to be comfortable living around humans.

paddy fields: a flooded area of land used for growing rice.

DID YOU KNOW?

Farmers in ancient China were some of the first in the world to **domesticate** livestock. Someone stepping onto a Chinese farm as early as 4000 BCE might have found chickens, cattle, pigs, and sheep.

PLANTING CROPS IN A ROW

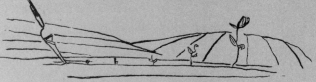

It seems like common sense to grow crops in a straight line. Surprisingly, this was not always the case in ancient China. Then in the third century BCE, a man named Master Lu wrote a book called *Master Lu's Spring and Autumn Annals*. He wrote, "if the crops are grown in rows, they will mature rapidly because they will not interfere with each other's growth." Rows not only made it easier to care for the crops, but farmers could also alternate different crops from row to row. They knew that just like people, even plants like to have their own personal space.

稻田
PADDY FIELDS

Right after the rice harvest in October, the farmers would plant winter crops in the fields, such as soybeans and wheat. Farmers had a very short window to do this crop change, sometimes as little as two weeks. They worked day and night to make sure the new winter crops were ready to go.

Usually, men were in charge of preparing the fields. But the whole family helped out when it came to planting the rice seedlings. Life revolved around the yearly farming cycle. The harvest itself might take just a few months, but farmers worked and prepared their land throughout the year. They only took breaks from their work for special occasions, such as Chinese New Year or one of the other festivals. There wasn't much time for a vacation if you were a farmer in ancient China!

WORDS TO KNOW

hoe: a garden tool used to weed or turn over soil.

alloy: a manmade combination of two or more metals.

foundry: a place where iron is produced.

trace harness: equipment that goes around a horse's chest so it can pull wagons or plows.

FARMING TOOLS

The Chinese were good with iron and developed many of the farming tools we still use today. Perhaps the most important tool they invented was the **hoe**. Simple hoes were used to plant crops in China as early as the fifth or sixth century BCE. By the first century BCE, Chinese farmers were using an improved design called the "swan-neck hoe" that could pull weeds without harming the plants. This hoe had several different blades that could be changed depending on what kind of farming was required.

鋤頭
HOE

This was a huge step forward. Instead of harvesting everything by hand, the Chinese could use these tools. This allowed them to have bigger and better harvests. Farmers began using the plow, called a *kuan*, around the third century BCE. The *kuan* had a sharp central piece that allowed farmers to dig more efficiently. It also had wings that flung soil away from the plow and helped reduce friction.

合金
ALLOY

The Chinese were some of the world's most talented bronze makers. Bronze is an **alloy**. Most bronze in ancient China was made by combining copper and tin. Depending on how they were mixed, the Chinese could create bronze in many different colors and hardnesses.

IRON

There was a great demand for iron tools in China. So the government set up **foundries**, or places where iron is produced, all across ancient China. Luckily, there was plenty of iron in China. Even common people used iron tools. In other places, like Europe, only the wealthiest people could afford iron.

In addition to farming tools, iron was also used to make all kinds of cooking tools, like cast-iron pots and pans. Iron was even used to make toys and giant, detailed sculptures.

THE WHEELBARROW

You have probably used a wheelbarrow to carry plants, dirt, or maybe even your friends! It wasn't used in Europe until sometime around the thirteenth century. But historians believe the wheelbarrow was actually invented around the first century BCE by a Chinese man named Kop Yu. Some designs placed the main wheel directly in the center of the wheelbarrow. Others located the wheel more towards the front, the way most wheelbarrows are today.

The Chinese used wheelbarrows for many things: farming, carrying goods, and even military purposes. Some people even attached sails to their wheelbarrows! It's noted that some of these wheelbarrows could travel more than 40 miles per hour over land or ice.

Bronze was incredibly useful. The metal could be made into coins, armor, cooking utensils, weapons, art, sculpture, and building materials.

Bronze was made by first creating a mold. This technique is called the "Lost Wax Method." Let's say that an artisan wanted to make a bronze sword. The artist would start by making a full-sized model of his sword out of clay. This is called the positive object. Once the model was finished, it was coated in a thin layer of rubber. After the rubber dried, the artisan put the model into a container and poured plaster over it. When the plaster molds were removed, the artisan would have two interlocking pieces with an empty space inside, in the shape of the original sword. This is called a negative.

Hot wax was then poured into each one of the molds. This created an exact copy of the original clay model in wax. The artisan made small holes in the wax mold, which would later let him pour bronze inside. Next, the artist covered the wax model with a mixture of plaster, sand and water. This was called an "investment."

When the investment and wax model were baked at a high temperature inside a kiln, the wax would melt and slide out through the holes. This is why the technique is called "Lost Wax." The process left only the investment behind. When the investment got hot enough, it became a rock-solid mold. Inside the mold was a new empty space in the shape of the sword. The artisan then poured very hot, molten bronze inside the final mold.

When the bronze cooled and the mold was pulled apart, you finally had your finished sword. Artisans could re-pour bronze into the sturdy mold dozens of times to make many swords. Each sword needed to be finished and detailed before it was ready to be presented to its new owner. No one said bronze casting was easy!

THE TRACE HARNESS

Tools made farming easier. But farmers could do even more once they learned how to "harness" the power of the horse. Ancient China was one of the first places in the world where horse harnesses were used to help plow fields and carry things long distances.

The earliest harnesses were tight around the horse's throat. Obviously, it's not a good idea to strangle the animal that's supposed to help you! By the fourth century BCE, farmers had started to use the **trace harness**. The trace harness was revolutionary because it placed most of the pressure on the horse's chest. Now horses could breathe better and exert more power.

With the earlier harness, two horses together could only pull about half a ton. But with a trace harness, just one horse was able to pull about a ton and a half. That's three times as much weight! By the third century BCE, farmers had created a collar harness with more padding to keep it from bothering the horse's skin.

MAKE YOUR OWN
BRONZE

SUPPLIES

- oil-based modeling clay
- heavy paper plates
- wax paper
- microwave oven
- petroleum jelly (like Vaseline)
- plaster of Paris
- bowl
- water
- spoon
- acrylic paint
- paint brushes
- shellac
- bamboo

You'll probably need to make a trip to an arts and crafts store for some of these supplies.

1 Take the clay out and work it for several minutes with your hands to loosen it up. If the clay is still very hard, flatten it into a circular disk. Make sure the disc is slightly larger than your hand. Place a piece of wax paper on top of the paper plate. Put the clay disk on top of the wax paper. Heat it in the microwave for between two and four minutes.

2 Take the clay out of the microwave. Be careful, as it may be very hot. Rub your hands with petroleum jelly (this might be a little gross! Don't worry—you can wash your hands off afterwards!). Push your palm into the clay disk so it leaves a deep imprint of your entire hand. Have your parents or a friend help push your fingers in so you get extra detail.

3 Repeat step 1 for a second piece of clay. Put your hand back in the imprint you already made with the first piece. Have a parent or a friend place the second clay disc on top of your hand. Make sure that your friend pushes down around the fingers to close in the spaces surrounding each finger. Seal all the parts where the two pieces of clay meet, otherwise the plaster will leak out in later steps.

FOUNDRY

4 Pull your hand out of the mold very carefully. Be sure not to break the seal or expand the space too much. You might have to spend a little time wiggling in order to do it right. Make minor repairs if you need to. If you really mess up, don't worry. The great thing about clay is it's not permanent! You can just repeat the steps and try again until you get a mold you like.

5 Following the instructions on the package, mix up the plaster of Paris. Usually, the mixture is two parts plaster to one part water. Stir it up until the mix is smooth and there are no more lumps.

6 Slightly turn your mold, and slowly pour the plaster into the mold. Let it sit for one hour.

7 After about an hour, peel back the clay from the dried plaster. Clean off any excess clay and plaster, especially between the fingers.

8 You can leave the hand unpainted and white, or use paint to decorate it however you want! When you've got a design that you're happy with, use some shellac to seal it.

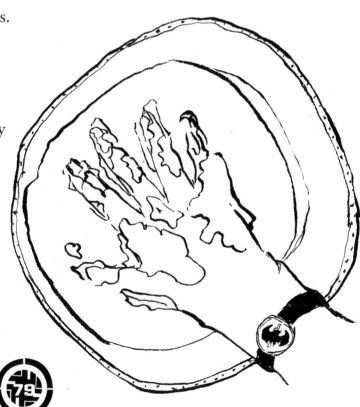

FOOD

One of China's greatest contributions to the world is its delicious food. Most Americans have eaten some kind of Chinese food. This American Chinese food is often very different from the food served in ancient China, or even from the food served in China today. But many dishes still share the same roots and histories.

You've probably eaten pasta, spaghetti, or even lo mein at some point. These are all different kinds of noodles. Over the last 2,000 years, noodles have become one of the most popular foods in the world. No one is really sure whether the Italians, the Chinese, or the Arabs invented noodles.

But in 2005 archaeologists discovered what they believe is the oldest-known bowl of noodles in the northwestern part of China. Even though the noodles were buried underneath more than 10 feet of dirt, they were still almost perfectly preserved. Talk about leftovers! To make ancient noodles, **millet** grain was ground up into flour. The flour was then turned into dough, which was pulled and stretched into the noodle's shape.

WORDS TO KNOW

millet: a fast-growing cereal plant grown in ancient China. Its seeds were used to make flour for foods like noodles.

brine water: salty water.

derrick: structure built from bamboo that drilled for salt water below the earth's surface.

evaporation: the process by which a liquid becomes a gas.

小米
MILLET

If you've ever eaten in a Chinese restaurant, you've probably eaten a fortune cookie. But fortune cookies did not exist in ancient China. There are many different stories about who invented the modern fortune cookie. One is that a man named David Jung came up with the cookie in the early 1900s. Jung was a Chinese immigrant in Los Angeles who created the Hong Kong Noodle Company. He'd place inspiring quotes inside his cookies and then pass them out to poor people hanging around his shop.

FORTUNE COOKIE MYTH

The origin of the fortune cookie probably goes back to the fourteenth century, during the Yuan Dynasty. It is believed that rebelling Chinese soldiers slipped messages into moon cakes, a traditional pastry, to communicate with each other. These rebels convinced the Mongolian ruler to distribute the cakes in honor of the ruler's long life. It was actually a trick and the message "revolt on the 15th of the 8th moon" was found inside. The moon cake messages may have organized the uprising that resulted in the new Ming Dynasty in 1368 CE.

DID YOU KNOW?

The nomadic people in China didn't farm. Instead, they lived off what naturally grew on the land. They were also experts at hunting and fishing.

Another story claims that a Japanese immigrant named Makoto Hagiwara invented the cookie in San Francisco. Hagiwara also designed the Japanese Tea Garden in San Francisco's Golden Gate Park. He might have passed out fortune cookies to people there. They were even featured in the 1915 World's Fair in San Francisco!

Fortune cookies became popular in the United States after WWII. Traditional Chinese meals do not end with dessert. But Americans are used to eating dessert at the end of a meal. So the fortune cookie offered a sweet, after-dinner treat.

Originally fortune cookies were made by hand. But in the 1960s a man named Edward Louie invented a fortune cookie machine that automatically slipped the fortune into the folded dough. Today, companies such as Wonton Food, Inc. in Queens, New York, ship out more than 60 million fortune cookies a month. That's a lot of good luck!

食物

FOOD

SALT

Salt was one of the most important foods in ancient China. Today, many people are lucky enough to have refrigerators that can store food for a long time. But in ancient China (and even today in some places), there was no such luxury. Salt was the most common way to preserve food, especially meats and vegetables.

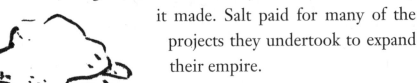

Because it was valuable, salt was also a good thing to trade. In fact, during the Han Dynasty, the emperors took over the entire salt-making business because they saw how much money it made. Salt paid for many of the projects they undertook to expand their empire.

There were several different ways to make salt. One of the easiest was to gather salt water in shallow pans and let it dry in the sun, leaving behind the salt residue. Sometimes salt makers poured salt water over sticks to increase the surface area. Then it didn't take as long for the water to dry off.

This was fine for people who lived near the sea. But people living inland needed another way to produce salt. They had to dig deep down into the earth to find salt water, or **brine water**. Sometimes this water could only be found several hundred or sometimes a thousand feet below the earth's surface.

How did the Chinese bring up water from that far down? As early as the first century BCE, engineers built giant towers out of bamboo called **derricks**. They were sometimes 180 feet tall! These towers looked like the oil drills you see today in places like Texas.

First, Chinese engineers hung a large iron drill from bamboo cables. Then, several men would jump up and down on a lever that pushed the drill down several feet at a time. It would take a lot of jumping to dig a deep well.

Once the brine water was reached, engineers put bamboo on the sides of the hole to make it strong. Most of the holes were at least 600 feet deep. But many averaged 3,000 feet deep and one was recorded as going as far as 4,800 feet below ground! Once the water was collected through a complex system of bamboo pipes, it was boiled in large cast iron **evaporation** pans until the water was gone and only the salt remained.

TEA

Drinking tea was an important part of life for every kind of person in ancient China, whether an emperor, farmer, poet, artist, merchant, or scholar. One legend says that tea was first "invented" in the year 2737 BCE. While Emperor Shen Nung was boiling hot water, a flower from the Camilla sinensis tea bush fell into his pot. This is the bush that almost all teas come from.

Whether or not the legend is true, we know for sure that around 350 CE, farmers began to grow tea. It soon became a very popular drink in ancient China, as well as a major cash crop. This means tea was sold to other countries where tea from China was considered rare and exotic. Usually, that meant it was also very expensive!

More than anything, tea was one of the most treasured and beloved products in ancient China. For at least 2,000 years, people in China have believed that tea has the power to cure some sicknesses and help keep the body healthy. But brewing tea was not just a simple, casual activity. Brewing, steeping, and serving tea the right way was a true art, with a very careful set of instructions.

A good pot of tea was not hard to find in ancient China. The same way many cities today have a coffeshop on every street corner, teahouses were all over the cities. Tea came in four main varieties—green, white, black and oolong (pronounced just like it looks!). There were also many occasions that would call for tea. A younger person offering tea to an elder was considered a sign of respect. A peasant might also offer tea to a higher-ranking noble, businessman, or court official. Tea was offered to someone as a way to apologize. It was a special gift that emperors offered foreign visitors. Family gatherings or ceremonies, especially weddings, would not be complete without tea for everyone.

MAKE YOUR OWN MOON CAKES

The Autumn Moon Festival is one of the oldest and most widely celebrated traditional Chinese holidays. Dating back as far as the Zhou Dynasty, it was a time to celebrate the end of the summer harvest and appreciate the beauty of the full moon. The Autumn Moon Festival usually falls on the 15th day of the 8th lunar month, usually in mid-to-late September. A fun and important tradition is to eat Chinese Moon Cakes. These are delicious, fruit-filled pastries that are easy to make and taste great with tea. Make sure you have permission to use the oven.

SUPPLIES

mixing bowls

2¾ cups flour

1 teaspoon baking soda

½ teaspoon baking powder

1½ cups sugar

1 cup softened butter

1 egg + 1 egg yolk

1 teaspoon vanilla extract

plastic wrap

cookie sheet

non-stick spray

1 cup fruit-flavored jam

oven

small bowl

pastry brush

1 Mix the flour, baking soda, and baking powder in a bowl. In a separate bowl, stir together the sugar and butter until they are smooth. Add the egg and vanilla. Little by little, stir the flour mixture into the sugar/butter mixture.

2 Rub some flour on your hands and shape the dough into a large ball. Wrap it with plastic and refrigerate for an hour.

3 Preheat your oven to 375 degrees Fahrenheit. Roll small balls of dough and place them onto the greased cookie sheet. With your thumb, make a hollow indentation in the center of each mooncake. Push down as deep as you can without puncturing the bottom of the dough.

4 Fill the hollows with jam. You will probably need a teaspoon or less in each. Beat the egg yolk in a small bowl and brush it over the mooncakes to give them a glazed finish. Bake the mooncakes for about 15 minutes, until the edges start to turn a light golden brown.

MAKE YOUR OWN CHINESE EGG

It's easy to make pasta, isn't it? Just boil some water, open up the box of pasta, empty it into the pot, and stir it around for 10 minutes. Of course, in ancient China, people couldn't buy pre-made dried noodles. They had to make noodles by hand. Back then, making noodles was a special art that had to be learned. This recipe should give you a taste of what it took to make noodles, from start to finish. And afterwards, you'll be able to impress your parents and friends with your new cooking skills!

1 Pour the flour into the large mixing bowl and carve out a little hole in the middle of the flour. Into the space you've carved out, add the eggs, salt, and oil.

2 Mix everything together with a fork (or your fingers!). Start by mixing everything in the middle of the hole, slowly bringing in more flour from the edges. Do this for a couple of minutes. Soon, you should be able to roll the dough up into a rough kind of ball. If there's any leftover ingredients on the side of the bowl, use a couple of drops of water to moisten them and help gather everything into one ball.

3 Spread some flour onto the cutting board. Take the dough out of the bowl and place it onto the board. Knead, or press into, the dough back and forth until it feels smooth. If it feels too sticky, it's okay to add some extra flour.

4 After you've done this for about 10 minutes, the dough should be shiny and smooth. Wrap it in a piece of wax paper. Let it sit for at least another 30 minutes.

5 After you've waited, take the dough out and separate it into two smaller balls. Put one of the balls onto the floured cutting board. Use the palm of your hand to shape it into a rectangular shape about one inch thick. Lightly cover the top with some more flour.

NOODLES

SUPPLIES

- 1½ cups unsifted flour
- large mixing bowl
- 3 eggs
- 1 teaspoon salt
- 1 tablespoon olive oil
- a few drops of water
- cutting board
- wax paper
- rolling pin
- knife
- large pot of water
- spoon

6 Use a rolling pin to flatten out the dough. Start by rolling away from you lengthwise. Then alternate and rotate the board, rolling across the width of the dough. Continue doing this and switching back and forth, until the dough is paper-thin. Dust the dough again with flour and let it sit another 10 minutes.

7 Now gently roll up the dough. Decide if you'd like thicker, fettucine-style noodles, or very thin, lo mein-style noodles. Depending on what kind of noodles you want, slice up along the length of the roll. It's okay to stretch the noodles to help get them extra thin.

8 Once you have cut all of the pieces, unroll them and place them back onto a piece of wax paper. Repeat the same process for the second ball of dough you saved earlier.

9 Now your noodles are ready to cook! Bring between six and eight quarts of salted water to a boil. Drop in the noodles. Stir once or twice to make sure the noodles aren't sticking together. Feel free to take a noodle out at any point to taste and make sure it is just right! Fresh, homemade noodles only need to cook for a couple of minutes. Drain the pasta and serve it with your favorite sauce. Noodles with just soy sauce or butter and parmesan taste great too!

BREW YOUR OWN CHINESE-STYLE TEA

1. Make invitations for your tea ceremony and send them to your friends. You can use the paper you created in the chapter on paper and sign it with the moveable type stamp you made in the chapter on writing. Drinking tea was a perfect chance to share art, poetry, or stories. Be sure to tell everyone you invite to bring along something to share.

2. Host your tea ceremony in a peaceful room with good feng shui. Adding flowers to the table or playing relaxing music are both nice touches. You might also host it outside if the weather is nice. The ideal spot to enjoy tea in ancient China was a pavilion right beside a lily pond—if you don't have either of those, a table in your backyard will work just fine!

3. Place a folded napkin on the table for each person. The folded napkin was a tradition thought to keep away bad *qi*, or bad energy.

4. Here's how to make the tea. This process works best with oolong tea, but can be used with any tea. First, boil a large

SUPPLIES

- paper and colored pencils
- flowers or other table decoration
- napkins
- oolong tea leaves *(available at most grocery or gourmet food stores)*
- kettle for boiling water
- small clay teapot
- teacups for your guests
- tray

pot of water. Use some of this hot water to rinse out your teapot. The water will be extremely hot, so be careful.

5. Fill about one-third of the teapot with the tea leaves. Fill the teapot about half-full with the hot water. Immediately pour the hot water into each one of the teacups you plan to use. This tea is not for drinking. Instead, it will warm and clean the teacups, preparing them for the actual tea.

AND HOST YOUR OWN
ANCIENT CHINESE TEA CEREMONY

6 Be sure that the teapot is sitting on the tray. And also, be sure the tray can hold spilled water, otherwise things might get a little messy. Now you're going to perform what's called a tea "infusion." Refill the teapot half full with more hot water. If you've run out of hot water, prepare another pot of boiling water. Then take all of the teacups and pour out the water directly into the teapot. This is part of the tradition and helps keep the teapot nice and warm.

7 Be sure not to let more than one minute pass from the time you've refilled the teapot. The first infusion should be very quick. Go ahead and pour tea into the teacups.

8 After you have poured tea for your guests, show them that the proper way for them to show respect and gratitude is to knock lightly on the table with their fingers. Hopefully, everyone chooses to drink your tea. Someone refusing to drink your tea is a sign of great disrespect!

9 If your guests want more tea, you can perform another "infusion." This time, let the tea steep a little longer, for about 90 seconds. Then repeat the same process. You should be able to perform at least three or four infusions. For each new infusion, let the tea steep 30 seconds or so longer than the time before.

10 In between infusions, your guests should share the games or stories they have brought. More important than anything else, be sure to have fun!

MAKE YOUR OWN
ICE CREAM

Many people believe that the very first ice cream was made in ancient China. But their ice cream was very different from the kind you like to have for desert today. Milk and dairy products were actually rare in ancient China (and are still rare today).

SUPPLIES

2 cups sugar

water

saucepan

grater

4–6 fresh oranges or about 2 cups of orange juice

knife

4-cup measuring cup

juice of 1 lemon

½ tsp vanilla extract

glass baking dish

freezer

blender

Instead, ice cream was more like a fruit sherbet, or sorbet. The recipes and styles of ice cream varied, but usually people would mix snow with different syrups or fruit extracts and juices. If you're lucky enough to have an ice cream maker, that will help for this activity. But if you don't, it's just as fun to make sorbet without one! You will need an adult to help with this activity.

1 Combine the sugar and 2 cups of water in a saucepan over high heat on the stove. Bring to a boil for about 2 minutes, stirring occasionally. When the sugar is dissolved, allow it to boil for another minute without stirring. Turn off the heat and set the syrup mixture aside.

2 Grate about 3 teaspoons of orange zest. Cut the oranges in half and squeeze about 2 cups of juice into the 4-cup measuring glass (or pour in the store-bought juice). Take out any seeds that fall in.

3 Add the syrup mixture, orange zest, and lemon juice. Stir everything together. Add enough water so that the total amount of liquid is 3½ cups. Stir in the vanilla extract. If you have an ice cream maker, place this mixture inside and follow the manufacturer's instructions.

4 If you don't have an ice cream maker, pour the mixture into the glass dish. Put the dish in the freezer for about an hour, or until it starts to get firm, but not frozen. Pour the sorbet into a blender and blend until it smooths out. Transfer the sorbet to a freezer-safe container. Place it into the freezer for another two hours. Enjoy!

TIME AND SPACE

In ancient China, some people spent their entire lifetimes trying to map out the stars and planets. Studying stars and planets wasn't just about science. Religion and politics were also influenced by the movements of the **celestial bodies**.

Today, the scientific study of the stars and universe is called **astronomy**. You can study it in school. Astronomers use math and science to help them understand the universe. **Astrology** is also the study of the stars and planets. But it is much less scientific and more spiritual than astronomy. Astrologists try to understand how the stars affect people.

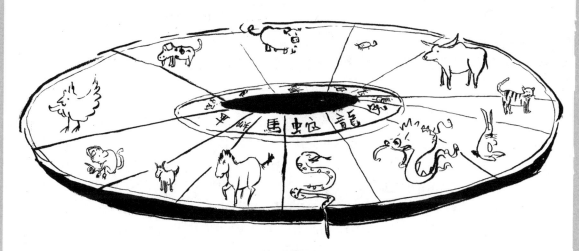

In ancient China, there wasn't much difference between astrology and astronomy. If something strange happened in the sky, the ancient Chinese thought great change was going to take place in the kingdom.

天體
CELESTIAL BODIES

天文
ASTRONOMY

Imagine what it would be like today if we used the stars and planets to tell us who the next president of the United States might be, or which country might win the next World Cup!

From an early time, the ancient Chinese noticed that the stars stayed in the same place relative to each other. They also saw that planets traveled in regular paths. There were lots of things they could see with the naked eye. But a stronger instrument was needed to chart and measure the stars and **constellations**. So the Chinese invented something called armillary spheres.

星象學
ASTROLOGY

The first armillary sphere was most likely invented by the Chinese astronomer Keng Shou-Ch'ang in 52 BCE. It was a circular ring, like a small hula-hoop. This ring was supposed to be the **equator**, or the imaginary line that goes around the middle of the earth. Like a ruler, the ring had carefully marked points on it. The astronomer would look through a tube placed in the middle of the ring to see the stars and sky. As he came upon each star, the astronomer would note where it appeared on the sphere.

星座
CONSTELLATION

DID YOU KNOW?

The word for stars in Chinese is *hengxing*, meaning "constant stars." The word for planets in Chinese is *xingxing*, meaning "moving stars." These words describe the stars and planets quite well. Stars are constant in the way they are positioned. The stars you see in the sky are like a giant map that changes depending on where you are in the world and when you look at the sky. But the planets move around on that map from night to night and month to month.

DID YOU KNOW?

Many royal buildings and palaces were built with the stars in mind. For example, the Temple of Heaven in Beijing has a square base that represents Earth. And its round ceiling is meant to be heaven.

Keng's design only had this one ring. A later design by Chang Heng, the same man who invented the first seismograph to record earthquakes, had other rings showing the paths of the moon, the planets, and sun. This allowed for very precise mapping of all the stars and constellations. Instead of seeing the sky as just a bunch of stars, astronomers now saw the sky as orderly and predictable.

Astronomers divided the sky into 28 different sections. Every star and constellation was assigned to one of the sections. This helped astronomers keep track of everything. Each section was called *hsiu* (pronounced "sue"). Each hsiu matched up with a new position of the moon as it moved across the sky.

赤道
EQUATOR

WORDS TO KNOW

celestial bodies: anything permanent in the sky, like the sun, stars, and planets and their moons.

astronomy: scientific study of the universe, especially the celestial bodies.

astrology: the study of how the movements of the sun, moon, and planets affect humans.

constellation: a group of stars that form a recognizable shape or pattern.

equator: an imaginary line that goes around the center of the globe.

solar calendar: a yearly calendar based on the cycles of the sun.

lunar calendar: a calendar based on the monthly phases of the moon.

WHAT ANIMAL ARE YOU?

For many people in the world, each year is just another big number. But in China, each year is named after one of 12 animals—the rat, ox, tiger, rabbit, dragon, snake, horse, sheep (or goat), monkey, rooster, dog, and pig (or boar). The list starts over every 12 years. Use this chart to figure out what year you were born in!

2000 ⇝ Dragon	1994 ⇝ Dog	
1999 ⇝ Rabbit	1993 ⇝ Rooster	
1998 ⇝ Tiger	1992 ⇝ Monkey	
1997 ⇝ Ox	1991 ⇝ Sheep (or goat)	
1996 ⇝ Rat	1990 ⇝ Horse	
1995 ⇝ Pig (or boar)	1989 ⇝ Snake	

Keeping track of time was just as important to the ancient Chinese as astronomy. Of course, the two go hand-in-hand with each other. Our calendar today is based on the fact that it takes 365 days for the earth to go around the sun. That's one year. The Chinese used this too, but their months are based on cycles of the moon. This is called a luni-solar calendar. In fact, the word for "month" in Chinese is *yue*, which also means "moon."

陽歷
SOLAR
CALENDAR

DID YOU KNOW?

For many years, people in Europe did not believe that sunspots existed. Sunspots are cooler areas on the surface of the sun. But ancient Chinese astronomers observed sunspots as early as the fourth century BCE.

The Chinese New Year begins sometime around late January or early February on the **solar calendar**. The months on the **lunar calendar** are 29 or 30 days long. That's how long the moon's cycle is.

But this means a year lasts only 354 days instead of 365! In order to even things out, an extra month was added to the lunar calendar every three years. This is what made it a luni-solar calendar. Think how you would feel if an extra month was added to the school year before summer!

陰曆
LUNAR
CALENDAR

SU SONG'S WATER CLOCK

Think about how you spend a normal day. If it's a school day, you might wake up at 7:30 in the morning and go to school at 8:00. You eat lunch at noon, then come home around 3:00. At 4:00 you go out to play basketball with your friends, and then eat dinner at 6:00. You do your homework at 7:00 and finally go to bed at 9:00. Sounds like a full day!

Today's busy schedules would not be possible without the invention of the mechanical clock. Ways to tell time have been around for a very long time. The ancient Babylonians used water clocks. And the ancient Egyptians, Greeks, and Romans all used sundials, which told time according to the position of the sun. These were all important inventions. But nothing compared to the amazing invention of the mechanical clock by Su Song in 1092.

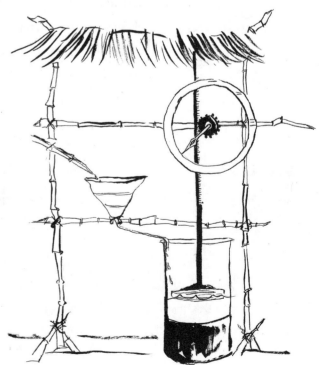

Unfortunately, the actual clock Su Song invented disappeared long ago. But historians, scientists, and archaeologists have built models of the clock based on Su Song's book *New Design for a Mechanized Armillary Sphere and Celestial Globe*. Su Song wrote about the design of his clock with an incredible amount of detail. Amazingly, his book has been preserved for over 900 years!

DID YOU KNOW?

You've probably used a chain-drive transmission hundreds of times and never even realized it! Your bicycle uses a chain-drive transmission. It is a system that uses a crank (a bike pedal) connected to a chain (a bike chain) to power a machine (a bicycle). It was originally invented in China in 976 by Chang Ssu-Hsun as part of his mechanical clock. But the chain-drive transmission became most famous a few years later when Su Song built his great clock.

Su Song's clock measured over 30 feet tall and needed its own room! It was made out of wood and bronze and had many mechanical gears. On the top, it had an armillary sphere for measuring the positions of the stars. At the bottom, it had a giant waterwheel that provided power for the moving parts of the clock. All the parts were connected by a chain drive, like a giant bike chain.

Because Su Song's clock used water for power, it was considered the first mechanical clock. It was even nicknamed "the Cosmic Engine." The giant water-wheel moved a complex system of bells and gongs that accurately told the time of day. Su Song's clock was in operation from 1092 until 1126, when it was taken apart and moved to Peking (modern-day Beijing). It ran there for several more years before it was taken apart for good.

almanacs

The Chinese believed that some days were very lucky and others were unlucky. People had books called almanacs to help them keep track of the meaning of each day. These were called *ri shun* in Chinese, meaning "day-books." *Ri shun* were some of the earliest books printed in ancient China.

MUSIC

The Chinese have one of the oldest musical traditions in the world. Music was not just for listening in ancient China. It was also an important part of religion and science. It was even used for measurement.

The most important instrument in ancient China was the bell. By 600 BCE, there were two different types of bells used in China. The *to* was a bell that faced upwards. The **chung** was a bell that faced downwards. These bells were usually made from bronze or iron. When it came to music, bells were not often used as instruments. Instead, they were used at the beginning of a piece to announce its start, or at the end of a piece to indicate its end.

WORDS TO KNOW

to: a bell that faced upwards.

chung: a bell that faced downwards.

pitch: the sound made by an instrument in a particular key.

scale: a series of musical notes arranged in ascending or descending pitch.

octave: the eight-step interval between notes in a scale.

shaman: someone who communicates with good and evil spirits.

zither: a stringed musical instrument.

And because bells were carefully made to ring at a specific **pitch**, they could be used to tune other musical instruments. Eventually, a 12-bell scale was created. This was the early beginning of our current **scale** within an **octave**.

If you've ever played the guitar or any stringed instrument, you know that a string makes a sound, or a pitch, when it's plucked. A regular piece of string will also make a sound, depending on how long it is. This is how bells were used as a measuring tool. First, a bell-maker would cut a certain length of string, pluck it, and listen to what pitch it made. He would then make a bell that matched that pitch exactly. For example, if the string were six feet long, the bell-maker would make a "six-foot" bell. Later, if someone wanted to cut a six-foot long piece of string, he would listen to that bell and only cut the string when its pitch matched the pitch of the bell. Bells could be easily carried and used anywhere!

MUSIC

MUSICAL SHAMANS

In ancient China there was such a thing as a musical **shaman**. A shaman is someone like a medicine man or a healer who can talk to good and evil spirits. Musical shamans used music to figure out the spiritual nature of people. For example, when an army went off to war, the shaman would blow on special pipes to figure out the *qi* of the opposing army. A weak sound might mean a weak army, and a strong sound might mean that the opposing army was well-equipped and strong.

AN ANCIENT ORCHESTRA

What do you think a 2,000-year-old orchestra looks like? In 1978 archaeologists discovered the tomb of Lord Yi of Zeng, who died around 433 BCE. Inside was an incredible array of ancient instruments. The instruments included **zithers** of all different sizes, bells, drums, and flutes. One set of bells had a total of 65 bells hanging from stands!

古箏
ZITHER

Bells were also used to measure in less complicated ways. Most commonly, they were used as scoops by farmers and merchants to measure grain. Because bells were a standard size, people could scoop grain and agree on the amount being purchased or sold.

The Chinese were also expert drum makers. They used drums for all kinds of special events, performances, and festivals. Percussion played a very important role in many ancient cultures. But Chinese percussion was different. They built drums that could be tuned, just like a piano! This was so the drum could match the pitch of other instruments that might be playing along with it.

The Chinese also understood that drums worked the same way as the human ear. Sound is actually just a series of vibrations. The Chinese knew that sound travels as waves through the air until it reaches the ear. And they knew

DID YOU KNOW?

Many bells were designed to produce two separate notes. If struck in the center, the bell would make one note. Struck at the side it would make a completely different note.

that sound waves strike the ear just as a drumstick strikes the face of a drum. All of this knowledge helped them to build even finer and more precise instruments.

GOING TO THE THEATER

The word *xi* (pronounced "shee") in Chinese means theater and the word *ju* (pronounced "joo") means drama. Chinese theater is very different from Broadway musicals and plays. It brings together many different art forms, including music, dance, costumes, and makeup, and sometimes even acrobatics.

One popular form of theater was called *zajus*, which was a kind of ancient Chinese variety show. In *zaju*, each actor might play up to four or five different roles. They might begin with dancing, then move on to acrobatics, a play or story, a bit of comedy, and finally a musical number to finish out the show.

Dancing in ancient China was not just for performers. It was a skill that well-educated people were expected to know. Someone who danced well was thought to have a strong connection between the body and the mind. Acrobatic performances in ancient China were the forerunners of modern circuses like Ringling Brothers and Cirque de Soleil. Acrobats would juggle multiple balls, do wild gymnastic feats, walk on tightropes, do tricks with animals, and perform amazing, death-defying stunts and feats of strength.

MAKE YOUR OWN CHINESE STRING INSTRUMENT

A real stringed instrument that was played in an ancient Chinese orchestra may have taken months, or even years to make. You don't have that kind of time, but you can make a simplified version of a Chinese fiddle, called an erhu. Unlike a guitar, the erhu has no frets. Instead, it is made of open, suspended strings and the erhu musician must know where each note lies.

SUPPLIES

wire clothes hanger

1 piece of string

hammer

nails

piece of wood, 2 inches by 4 inches, 3 feet long

1 acoustic guitar string

1 Tie the end of one of the strings to the bottom corner of the clothes hanger. Tie the other end to the opposite side. Make sure that the string is tight enough that it makes the hanger bend and pushes its bottom end inwards. When you "pluck" the string it should make a low tone.

2 Hammer a small nail to one end of the 2 by 4. Attach the loop of the acoustic guitar string around the nail. Attach a second nail to the other end of the 2 by 4. Wrap the loose end of the guitar string around the nail so that it is tight.

3 You can now use your clothes hanger as a bow to slide across the stationary string. It should create a buzzing pitch. This copies the way that many Chinese stringed instruments worked, like the erhu. If you want a higher pitch, pull the string tighter. For a lower pitch, make it looser.

MAKE YOUR OWN CHINESE PUPPET

Puppetry was another major form of art and entertainment in ancient China. Historians think that the earliest puppets may have dated all the way back to the Shang Dynasty, between the sixteenth and eleventh centuries BCE!

Archaeologists have found porcelain figurines buried with rulers from that time. For many centuries, puppets may have only been used to place in tombs alongside the dead. But by the Tang Dynasty (618–907 CE), puppets were used in performances for the living. Over the years, puppets became more and more sophisticated. Many puppets were designed to look as lifelike as possible. Artisans would spend months just working on the details of the puppet's face or on its clothing. They were true works of art. And puppet shows were not just for children. People of all ages enjoyed watching dramas, comedies, and tragedies performed with puppets. Puppeteers were also masters of movement, who could make the puppet's motions seem just like a human's.

1. Design the puppet's head and face. If you have googly eyes, attach them to the Styrofoam ball with glue. Use the magic markers to color in other features on the face. Remember, the best puppets in ancient China looked as lifelike as possible!

2. Make hair for your puppet. Cut strands of yarn to the length you'd like your puppet's hair to be. Attach it to the Styrofoam head using the glue. For your puppet's interior skeleton, stick the Styrofoam head on top of one of the BBQ skewers.

SUPPLIES

2 Styrofoam balls

googly eyes *(available at craft stores)*

glue gun or craft glue

magic markers

yarn

2 BBQ bamboo or wooden skewers

scissors

colored felt

needle and thread

sequins, glitter, glue, buttons, other decorations

rubber band

3 In ancient China, puppets wore elegant robes or gowns. The colors were also very bright, because it would catch an audience's eye during a performance. To make clothing for your puppet, you'll need to cut out pieces of felt, one for the front, and one for the back. Each piece should be about the size of a piece of 8½-by-11-inch paper. Use the markers to trace an outline of your clothing on each piece of felt before you cut it. The clothing should just be upper-body clothing, in the shape of a shirt or robe. Use the sewing needle and thread to attach the front and back of the clothing to each other.

4 Decorate it with gold glitter glue, sequins, or any other details you'd like to add. The opening for the neck should be quite small. Don't make pants or a spot for the two legs—otherwise you won't be able to fit your hand through the bottom! Slide the second Styrofoam ball into the bottom of the clothing. This is the body.

5 Push the skewer from the head down into the body until it almost meets the head. Make sure the neckline of your clothing is resting on the lower Styrofoam ball. Take the rubber band and wrap it around the outside of the clothing, so it holds the clothing tightly to the lower ball. Push the second skewer into the bottom of the body.

6 Your puppet is ready for its first performance! You can hold the puppet from the bottom of the skewer, or place your hands inside each one of the puppet's arms to make it move.

CHANG HENG'S SEISMOGRAPH

The threat of earthquakes has always been a major fear for the Chinese people. Today, China has cities with giant skyscrapers and millions of people living close together. An earthquake could be catastrophic. Even in ancient China, when the cities were smaller and there were fewer people, earthquakes could still be deadly and destructive.

A very smart man named Chang Heng knew there wasn't much people could do to stop earthquakes. But he also felt that people weren't helpless, either. He thought that if the royal court could record an earth-quake when it hit, the emperor could get food and other resources to the trouble spot much quicker.

Chang Heng was a talented sci-entist, inventor, mathematician, and royal astronomer for the Han Dynas-ty in the second century CE. At this time, most people still believed that the world was flat! But Chang Heng published a book called *Spiritual Constitution of the Universe*. In this book, he said the world was a "spherical ball suspended in infinite space." He also said that the world was made up of nine different continents. He is regarded as the first person to use north/south and east/west grid lines to divide the earth. These lines are called **latitude** and **longitude**. Talk about being ahead of his time!

緯度
LATITUDE

經度
LONGITUDE

In 132 CE, Chang came up with the world's very first **seismograph**, or earthquake detector. The main piece of the seismograph was a giant bronze urn, or jar, that measured almost six feet across. The outside of the urn was decorated with beautiful animal and flower patterns along with poetry and famous sayings.

Inside the urn was a weighted **pendulum**. A pendulum is the part of a clock that swings back and forth. The seismograph was placed on a sensitive table that could detect movement. If an earthquake struck near or far, it would cause the pendulum to swing in the direction of the earth's movement.

DID YOU KNOW?

Chinese scientists left detailed records of the location, strength, and damages caused by earthquakes as early as 780 BCE. In fact, China's written record of earthquakes is the oldest in the world!

地震儀
SEISMOGRAPH

Bronze dragons were attached to eight different sides of the urn. Each dragon had a small bronze ball held inside its mouth. Below each dragon was a small bronze frog that also had an open mouth. If the movement of the pendulum was strong enough, it would activate a pin mechanism inside the jar. The pin would then knock one of the balls out of the dragon's mouth and into the frog's mouth. Someone could tell which direction the earthquake came from, depending on which frog caught the ball.

擺錘
PENDULUM

At first, nobody believed that Chang Heng's strange device could work. Then one day, a ball fell from the mouth of one of the dragons, even though no one in the emperor's palace felt a tremble. A couple of days passed and then a messenger arrived with news that an earthquake had hit the town of Lung-Hsi. After that, everyone believed in the power of Chang Heng's amazing seismograph.

Chang Heng's seismograph was used in China until about the seventh century. Then it was lost. It was not until 1703 that the first modern seismograph was built in the Europe by a man named de la Hautefeuille. Chang Heng was many centuries ahead of his time!

WORDS TO KNOW

latitude: imaginary lines dividing the earth running east to west, or horizontally, parallel to the equator.

longitude: imaginary lines dividing the earth running north to south, or vertically, through the North and South Poles.

seismograph: a device used to detect earthquakes.

pendulum: a weight hung from a fixed point that swings back and forth due to gravity.

MAKE YOUR OWN MODEL SEISMOGRAPH

In this activity, you'll have a chance to build a replica of Chang Heng's original seismograph. Your model might not be able to detect earthquakes, but it will give you an idea of the design behind this incredible instrument.

SUPPLIES

large plastic food jar
permanent markers
utility knife
8 plastic spoons
green Sculpey clay
8 marbles
Elmer's glue
8 paper cups

1 Stand the jar upright and remove the lid. Use a permanent marker to mark 8 spots evenly spaced around the jar, about an inch below the top. Have an adult help you use the utility knife to cut a small slit in the plastic jar at each spot that you've marked. Each slit should be just wide enough so that the flat end of one of the spoons can fit through it.

2 Draw designs on the outside of the jar with the permanent markers. In ancient China a real seismograph may have had poetry or a beautiful landscape engraved on the sides. Use your imagination to decorate your own seismograph.

3 Make eight small dragon heads with the Sculpey clay to decorate the spoons. Their mouths should be big enough to hold a marble. Either sculpt the dragons and then attach them to each spoon, or make the dragon directly on the spoon. Place a marble inside each one of the dragon's mouths.

4 Slide the flat end of one of the spoons through one of the slits. Clump a piece of Sculpey clay to the end of the spoon that's sticking inside the jar. It should keep the spoon from sliding out of the hole. Repeat this step for the other seven spoons. If your spoons slide out of the holes, use a little Elmer's glue to help hold it in place. Put the lid back on your seismograph.

5 To make the marble-catching frogs, cover each paper cup with Sculpey clay. Use the cup as a base and make a frog decoration out of clay around the cup. Place the cups below each dragon and you have your very own seismograph.

NUMBERS

一 二 三 四 五
六 七 八 九 十

1 - 10

Can you imagine what life would be like without numbers? Well, math didn't just appear out of thin air. Brilliant thinkers thousands of years ago came up with the ideas that shape the way we understand math today. Of course, mathematics wasn't invented in ancient China. People from many different cultures have made important contributions. But the Chinese did come up with many math ideas that we use today.

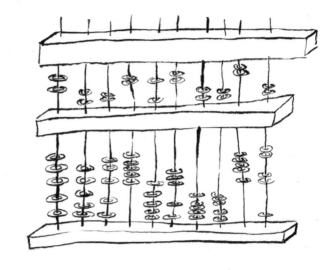

Some ancient cultures wrote numbers using the alphabet, which usually meant that there would be many more than 10 numbers. But the Chinese used special symbols for their numbers. Instead of creating a new symbol for "11" or "12," the Chinese came up with a system that combines the numbers from zero to nine. This was a revolutionary idea that formed the foundation for the **decimal system**.

The decimal system goes at least as far back as the Shang Dynasty in the fourteenth century BCE. We still use the it today. With this system we can write any number we want using only the symbols 1, 2, 3, 4, 5, 6, 7, 8, 9 and 0, plus a decimal point if needed. Other math systems before the decimal system had separate characters for each number beyond 9. So instead of using a 1 and a 0 to write ten, there were whole new symbols altogether for 10, 11, 12, 13, etc. That means if you wanted to count to 1,000, you'd have to memorize 1,000 different characters! It was not the most practical system!

算盤

ABACUS

At first, the Chinese used **counting rods** to do math. Counting rods were small bars that could represent any number and any fraction. They worked fine for simple math, but they were much too slow for harder problems. People needed to carry over 200 counting rods if they wanted to count correctly!

WORDS TO KNOW

decimal system: a number system using groups of ten.

counting rods: early tools used for making calculations in ancient China.

abacus: an instrument for performing calculations by sliding beads along rods.

tangrams: an ancient Chinese game using seven shapes to make various pictures.

hexagon: a six-sided shape.

DID YOU KNOW?

The Chinese were one of the first civilizations to understand the idea of zero. It might not seem like much, but the math, science, and physics of today would not exist without zero. At first, the Chinese used a blank space for zero when using their counting rods. Many years later, they replaced the blank space with an actual character for zero.

The answer to this problem was the **abacus**. No one knows for sure if the abacus was invented in China. But we do know that it was invented somewhere between 1000 and 500 BCE and was used throughout ancient China.

The abacus was one of the most important tools for merchants, astronomers, and mathematicians. It was usually about eight inches high. Depending on how the abacus would be used (and its owner's hand size!), it could come in many different widths.

The abacus had two decks separated by a bar. Rows on the upper deck had two wooden beads. Rows on the lower deck had five beads. Each bead on the upper deck equaled five units. Each bead on the lower deck equaled one unit. Numbers are indicated by sliding the beads toward the bar. It's easiest to use the abacus for counting. But with a little practice, it can also be used for addition, subtraction, multiplication, and division. It even works for square roots and cube roots! Think you're ready to give up your calculator?

NEGATIVE NUMBERS

It's always nice to have money. But the world isn't perfect and sometimes we owe money. As early as the second century BCE, the Chinese had a solid understanding of negative numbers, or a minus sign. This was hundreds of years before Europeans discovered the same idea. The Chinese used black rods on the counting board for negative numbers. Positive numbers were shown with red rods.

MAKE YOUR OWN ABACUS

With your own abacus, you can open up your own shop in an ancient Chinese marketplace! Just make sure you know how to use your new abacus. If you overcharge your customers, you might go out of business very quickly!

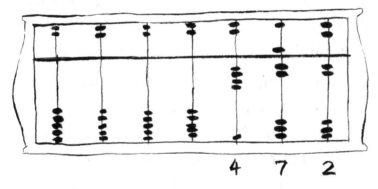

4   7   2

1. Use the ruler to outline three, 11-by-2-inch pieces of Styrofoam insulation. Cut out all three pieces with the scissors or utility knife. With your pen or pencil, use the ruler to make a mark every one inch on all three pieces of Styrofoam. Poke the barbeque skewers through one of the Styrofoam pieces at each mark.

2. To make the smaller upper deck, place two metal washers on each end of the skewer, then seal them in by sliding the skewers right through the second piece of Styrofoam at the marks you made. To make the larger lower deck, place five metal washers on the end of each skewer, then seal it shut it in same fashion with the remaining piece of Styrofoam.

3. You may want to reinforce the joints with some tape or glue to make sure everything holds in place. If you have extra Styrofoam, you can create two extra side walls for more strength.

MAKE YOUR OWN TANGRAMS

People of all ages in ancient China played a mathematical game called tangrams. **Tangrams** works a little bit like a jigsaw puzzle. But tangram pieces, called "tans," don't have pictures printed on them. Instead, they are usually solid colors. You can make all kinds of shapes and figures when they're put together. For example, tans can be arranged to form a dog, or a running man, or a tree.

SUPPLIES

piece of cardboard
or heavy-duty
construction paper

protractor

pen or pencil

ruler

scissors

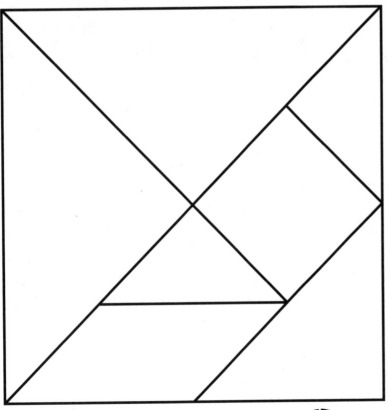

I   For a quick and easy way to make tangrams, you can trace or photocopy the illustration to the left. If you're more adventurous, you will need to start by drawing a perfect square with sides about 8 inches long. Draw the top side of the square. Then use the protractor to measure out all four perfect 90-degree angles and finish the outer square. Label the sides A, B, H, J, like the illustration on the next page.

2 Now use your ruler to connect corners B and H. Also draw a light line connecting corners A and J. Label the point where these two lines intersect, "D."

3 Measure halfway between corners B and J and mark that point "E." Measure halfway between corners H and J and mark that point "I." Now connect these two halfway points.

4 Measure halfway between E and I and mark that point "G." Connect point G with point D (this line should already be lightly penciled in). Erase the remaining part of the line connecting G to J.

5 Measure halfway between points B and D. Label this point "C." Connect C to E.

6 Measure halfway between points D and H. Label this point "F." Connect points F and G.

7 Now your outlines should be complete. Make sure it looks like the diagram. Cut out each of the shapes with your scissors. Be sure to cut on the lines! Go online to find shapes to make with your tangrams. There are lots of web sites with puzzles for you to solve.

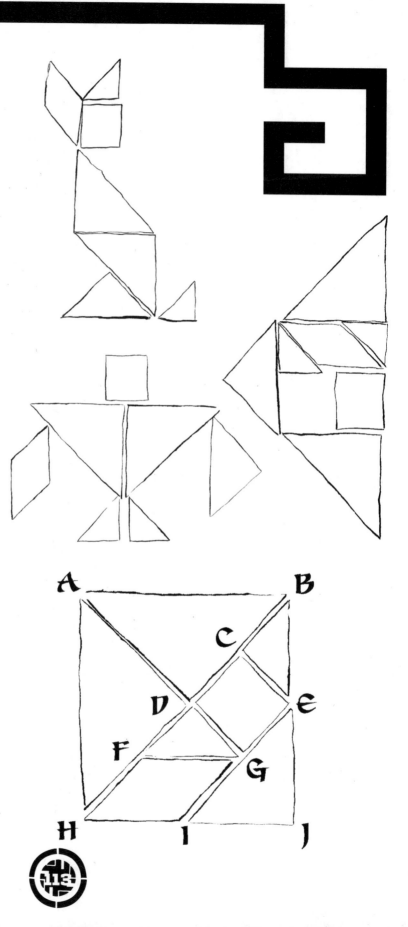

MAKE YOUR OWN PAPER SNOWFLAKE

In this activity, you'll learn how to make paper snowflakes. You can use paper you've bought from the store. Or, you can try using paper you made from the earlier paper-making activity. Follow the directions shown in the pictures to make your first snowflake. Then experiment with other ideas to make many different snowflakes.

SUPPLIES

pieces of square paper

scissors

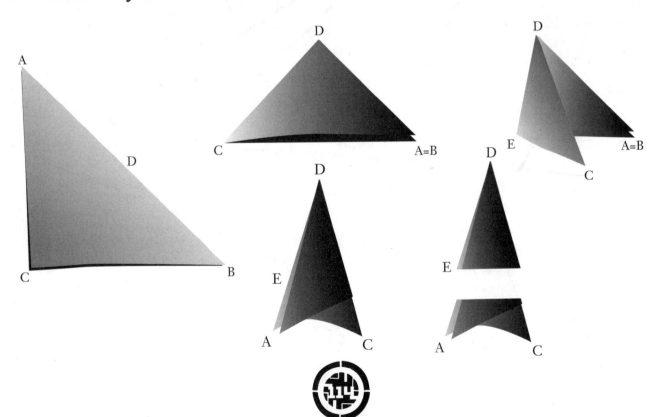

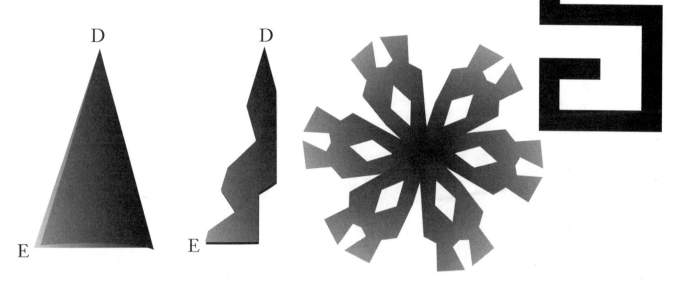

SNOWFLAKES AND HEXAGONS

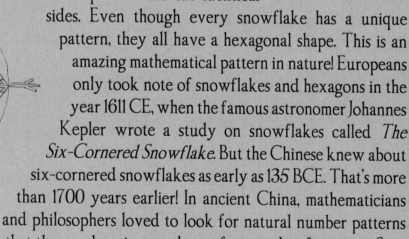

Have you ever tried to catch snowflakes on your hand? If you take a close look at a snowflake before it melts, you'll see that it's shaped like a **hexagon**. This means that its pattern has six identical sides. Even though every snowflake has a unique pattern, they all have a hexagonal shape. This is an amazing mathematical pattern in nature! Europeans only took note of snowflakes and hexagons in the year 1611 CE, when the famous astronomer Johannes Kepler wrote a study on snowflakes called *The Six-Cornered Snowflake*. But the Chinese knew about six-cornered snowflakes as early as 135 BCE. That's more than 1700 years earlier! In ancient China, mathematicians and philosophers loved to look for natural number patterns in nature. People believed that the number six was the perfect number for water. So it only made sense that frozen water, or snow, would take the shape of a hexagon.

六角形

HEXAGON

GLOSSARY

abacus: an instrument for performing calculations by sliding beads along rods.

acupuncture: a form of healing that involves sticking needles into certain points on the body to restore the proper flow of *qi*.

alloy: a manmade combination of two or more metals.

ashi: the points on the body where acupuncture needles affect the flow of *qi*.

astrology: the study of how movements of the sun, moon, and planets affects humans.

astronomy: scientific study of the universe, especially the celestial bodies.

asymmetrical: a design that does not look the same on both sides.

batten: bamboo or wooden supports that divide a sail into several sections.

battering ram: a huge, heavy log carried by many people. When used with force, it can break down large walls.

bow: the front of a ship.

brine water: salt water.

bulkhead: a large partition or section inside of a ship. These were often watertight.

calligraphy: the art of beautiful writing.

cartography: The science of making maps.

cavalry: an army of soldiers on horseback.

celestial bodies: anything permanent in the sky, like the sun, stars, and planets.

Chinese Civil Service Exam: a difficult exam that tested knowledge of Confucianism, literature, history, writing, and even morals.

chung: a bell that faced downwards.

coarse: a surface that feels harsh or rough.

cocoon: a silky protective case spun by young insects.

Confucianism: a set of religious and social ideas created by a man named Confucius, who lived from 551 to 479 BCE.

constellation: a group of stars that form a recognizable shape or pattern.

contour: the shape or structure of something.

coordinates: numbers that are used to determine the position of a point.

counting rods: early tools used for making calculations in ancient China.

decimal system: a number system using groups of ten.

derrick: structure built from bamboo that drilled for salt water below the earth's surface.

divination: the use of superstition and omens by a healer to help diagnose a patient's illness and predict future recovery.

domesticate: to raise animals to be comfortable living around humans.

dynasty: a powerful family or group that rules for many years. Some ancient Chinese dynasties continued for several hundred years and some were very short.

equator: an imaginary line that goes around the center of the globe.

evaporation: the process by which a liquid becomes a gas.

fibers: the smaller pieces or threads of a material that has been broken down.

foundry: a place where iron is produced.

gate locks: an engineering feature on canals that helps raise or lower boats from one level of water to another. It helps make a waterway easier to navigate.

ginseng: a plant grown in China that has many different health benefits.

grid: a series of evenly spaced horizontal and vertical lines.

hemp: a plant that grows in Asia. Its fibers are used to make many materials.

hexagon: a six-sided shape.

hoe: a garden tool used to weed or turn over soil.

hull: the main body of a ship.

indigo: a plant used to make dark blue dyes.

irrigation: a technique of transporting water through canals to water crops.

jade: a beautiful, slightly clear green stone, one of the most prized natural materials in China. It has been used for all kinds of applications, mostly jewelry and art, for over 6,000 years.

jingmai: channels, or highways, that run through the body. The *qi* was believed to move through each channel in a certain pattern.

junk: a style of flat-bottomed sailboat that was very popular in ancient China.

latitude: imaginary lines dividing the earth running east/west, parallel to the equator.

longitude: imaginary lines dividing the earth north to south, or vertically, through the North and South Poles.

loom: a large, frame-like machine that stretches fibers and allows the weaver to stitch, or twist, them together.

lunar calendar: a calendar based on the monthly phases of the moon.

Mandate of Heaven: the idea that China's emperor got his power straight from heaven. That meant people trusted him to rule over just about everything, from the economy and government to trade and religion. That power could also be taken away if the emperor did not use it for the good of his people.

matting: a rough material made from natural fibers like grass. This was used for sails.

metallurgy: the study and understanding of the properties of different metals.

millet: a fast-growing cereal plant grown in ancient China. Its seeds were used to make flour for foods like noodles.

monastery: a place where monks devoted their lives to prayer and religious study.

moveable type: an important advance in printing where individual characters could rearranged easily, allowing books to be printed more cheaply.

moxibustion: a healing technique that involves burning an herb called "mugwort" right above specific energy points on the body.

nomads: people that move from one place to another, instead of living in one place.

octave: the eight-step interval between two notes in a scale.

omen: a sign of something to come in the future.

paddy fields: a flooded area of land used for growing rice.

pendulum: a weight hung from a fixed point that swings back and forth due to gravity.

pictogram: a written symbol that represents a word or object.

pitch: the sound made by an instrument in a particular key.

porcelain: a fine, smooth, white clay material created by extreme heat.

prism: a clear triangular-shaped object that can reflect the full color range of the rainbow.

qi: an invisible energy that flows through the entire universe.

rammed earth: a building process that involves compressing a mixture of sand, gravel, and clay into a solid wall.

relief maps: three-dimensional maps that show people exactly how the land and mountains looked, but on a smaller scale.

rudder: a piece of wood attached to the back of a ship used for steering.

rural: areas in the countryside.

scale: a series of musical notes arranged in ascending or descending pitch.

seismograph: a device used to detect earthquakes.

shaman: someone who communicates with good and evil spirits and the spiritual world.

shi: heated stones that are sometimes used in place of acupuncture needles.

silt: fine-grained soil rich in nutrients, often found at the bottom of rivers or lakes.

solar calendar: a yearly calendar based on the cycles of the sun.

stern: the back of a ship.

stirrup: a metal ring with a flat bottom attached to a leather strap. Stirrups hang from both sides of a riding saddle on a horse. Riders put their feet in the stirrups to give them greater control.

superstitions: beliefs that deal with non-scientific things, like good luck and bad luck.

symmetrical: a building or design that looks identical on both sides, like a mirror image.

tangrams: an ancient Chinese game using seven shapes to make various pictures.

terracotta: earthen clay used as a building material, for pottery and for sculptures, like the Terracotta Army.

terrain: a specific area of land and its natural features (hilly, swampy, dry).

to: a bell that faced upwards.

topography: the natural features of the land, especially as they appear on a map.

trace harness: equipment that goes around a horse's chest so it can pull wagons or plows.

two-dimensional: something that is flat, like a map, a television screen, or a chalkboard.

UNESCO: the United Nations Educational, Scientific and Cultural Organization. It supports cultural projects across the world and also helps preserve historic and ancient sites.

wood-block printing: a printing process where images are carved in reverse into a large piece of wood, then inked and pressed onto paper.

wood pulp: a fluffy material that results when wood is broken down.

World Heritage Site: a special site named by UNESCO that deserves to be restored or preserved for future generations, like the Great Wall of China.

yaw: the act of turning a ship.

yin and yang: a belief that the world is balanced out by opposing forces.

zhen: the needles used in acupuncture.

zither: a stringed musical instrument.

RESOURCES

BOOKS

Baldwin, Robert F. *Daily Life in Ancient and Modern Beijing*. Runestone Press, 1999.

Dutemple, Lesley A. *The Great Wall of China*, Lerner Publications Company, 2003.

Greenberger, Robert. *The Technology of Ancient China*. Rosen Publishing Group, 2006.

Harvey, Miles. *Look What Came From China*. Franklin Watts, 1998.

Roberts, J.A.G. *A Concise History of China*. Cambridge: Harvard University Press, 1999.

Shaughnessy, Edward J. *China: Empire and Civilization*. Oxford University Press, 2000.

Temple, Robert. *The Genius of China: 3,000 Years of Science, Discovery and Invention*. London: Prion Books Limited, 1998.

Williams, Suzanne. *Made in China: Ideas and Inventions from Ancient China*. Berkeley: Pacific View Press, 1996.

WEBSITES

"The History of the Fortune Cookie," by Borgna Brunner. http://www.infoplease.com/spot/fortunecookies.html

http://www.taichiacademy.com/formsandmovements.htm

http://www.skratch-pad.com/kites/make.html

http://www.lldkids.com/kids/projects/compass.html

http://www.tylermuseum.org/press_Treasures.htm

http://www.cdkitchen.com/recipes/recs/101/Homemade_Egg_Noodles9978.shtml

http://news.nationalgeographic.com/news/2005/10/1012_051012_chinese_noodles_2.html

http://www.bellaonline.com/articles/art29812.asp

http://wildlifeart.org/Foundry/index2.html

http://www.diynetwork.com/diy/ca_crafts_projects/article/0,2041,DIY_13721_2273426,00.html

http://www.dsokids.com/2001/dso.asp?PageID=101

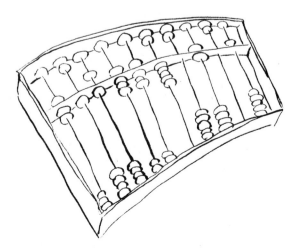

INDEX

A

abacus, 109, 110, 111
acrobatics, 100
activities
    abacus, 111
    animated terracotta army, 36–38
    bronze foundry, 78–79
    Chinese egg noodles, 86–87
    Chinese junk, 64–65
    compass, 63
    feng shui house, 14–15
    ice cream, 90
    ink, 29
    jade *bi* jewelry, 47
    kite, 40–42
    mini-yurts, 12–13
    moon cakes, 85
    moveable type, 26–28
    paper, 19–21
    puppets, 102–103
    relief map, 56–57
    seismograph, 107
    snowflakes, 114–115
    string instrument, 101
    suspension bridge, 54–55
    t'ai ch'i, 71
    tangrams, 112–113
    tea ceremony, 88–89
    terracotta clay army, 39
acupuncture, 67–68, 69
agriculture, 5, 72–77
alloys, 74, 75. *See also* bronze
almanacs, 96
animals, 2–3, 32, 33, 73, 77, 94
animation, 36–38
apothecaries, 9
architecture, 6, 8–15
armillary spheres, 92–93, 96
art, 7, 43–44, 102
Art of War, The (Sun Tzu), 35
ashi, 69, 70
astrology/astronomy, 91–95
asymmetry, 10–11
Autumn Moon Festival, 81, 85

B

bagua, 14–15
battens, 60
battering rams, 32
Beijing, vi, 6, 10, 93
bells, 97–99
bi, 44, 47
Bi Sheng, vi, 25
books, 23–25, 27, 95, 96. *See also* writing
borders of China, 6–7
bow, 59
bridges, 49, 50, 54–55
brine water, 81, 83
bronze, 32–33, 52, 75–79, 96, 97, 105–106
bulkheads, 60–61

C

calendars, 73, 93, 94–95
calligraphy, 3
canals, 49, 51
cartography, 53. *See also* maps
cavalry, 32, 33
celestial bodies, 91, 93
chain-drive transmission, 96
Chang Heng, v, 52, 53, 93, 104–107
Chinese Civil Service Exam, 23, 25
Chinese junks, 59–60, 64–65
Chinese New Year, 74, 94
chung, 97–98
cities, 5–6, 8–10, 104. *See also* Forbidden City; Xi'an
claymation, 36
clocks, 95–96
cocoons, 44, 45–46
coins, 51–52
colors, 15, 31, 46
compasses, 62–63
Confucianism, 22, 23
Confucius, iv, 2–3, 24
cong, 44
constellations, 92, 93
contours, 56
cookies, fortune, 81–82

coordinates, 53
counting rods, 109
crops, 73–74. *See also* farming
crossbow, 32

D

dancing, 100
death points, 68
decimal system, 109
derricks, 81, 83
divination, 70
doctors, 69–70. *See also* health
domesticated animals, 73. *See also* horses
double-cropping, 73
drums, 99–100
Dynasties. *See also* Periods
    definition of, 5
    Five, the, vi
    Han, v, 53, 59, 82
    Ming, vi, 9, 10, 61, 81
    Qin, v
    Qing, 7, 10
    Shang, iv, 4, 6, 102, 109
    Song, vi, 62
    Tang, vi, 102
    Yuan, vi, 81
    Zhou, iv, 5, 85

E

earthquakes, 52, 104–107
education, 22–24
emperors. *See also* Dynasties; palaces
    Khubilai Khan, vi
    Mandate of Heaven and, 5
    Qin Shi Huangdi, v, 9, 34, 50, 52
    Shen Nung, 84
    Yellow Emperor, 67
    Zhou kings, iv, 5
entertainment, 97–103
equator, 92, 93
erhu, 101
evaporation, 81, 83
exercise, 69, 71
explorers, 58–62

F

farming, 5, 72–77
feng shui, 11, 14–15
fibers, 16–19, 46, 60
fireworks, 31
Five Dynasties, the, vi
food, 80–90
Forbidden City, vi, 6, 10
fortune cookies, 81–82
foundries, 74, 75, 78–79

G

gardens, 11
gate locks, 51
ginseng, 67, 68
government, 9–10.
    See also Dynasties;
    emperors; military; Periods
Grand Canal, 51
Great Wall of China, v, vi, 9
grids, 53, 105
gunpowder, 31

H

halberd, 31
Han Dynasty, v, 53, 59, 82
harnesses, 74, 77
healers, 68, 70. *See also* shamans
health, 66–71
hemp, 17, 18
hengxing, 92
herbs, 9, 67–69
hexagons, 109, 115
hoes, 74, 75
horses, 2–3, 32, 33, 77, 94
houses. *See* architecture
hsiu, 93
hulls, 59

I

ice cream, 90
indigo, 31, 48, 49
ink, 29
instruments, musical, 97–101
iron, 31, 32–33, 49, 62, 75, 97
irrigation, 73

J

jade, 43–45, 47
jewelry, 43–44, 47
jingmai, 67
ju, 100
Jung, David, 81
junks, 59–60, 64–65

K

Keng Shou-Ch'ang, v, 92–93
Kepler, Johannes, *The Six-
    Cornered Snowflake*, 115
Khubilai Khan (emperor), vi
kites, 34–35, 40–42
Kleenex, 21
Kop Yu, 76
kuan, 75

L

latitude, 105, 106
livestock, 73. *See also* horses
longitude, 105, 106
Longshan people, 73
looms, 44, 46
Lost Wax Method, 76–77
Louie, Edward, 82
lunar (luni-solar) calendar,
    93, 94–95

M

Magic Canal, 51
Makoto Hagiwara, 82
Mandate of Heaven, 5
maps, 52, 53, 56–57, 92–93.
    See also latitude
markets/marketplaces, 9, 48, 51.
    See also trade
martial arts, 68, 69, 71
*Master Lu's Spring and Autumn
    Annals* (Master Lu), 74
mathematics, 108–115
matting, 60
measurements, 51, 52–53, 98–99
medicine, 9, 68–69.
    See also health
merchants, 48–53, 56.
    See also trade

M

mercury poisoning, 56
metallurgy, 32.
    See also alloys; bronze; iron
Middle Kingdom, 5
military, 30–35, 81.
    See also weapons
millet, 80–81
Ming Dynasty, vi, 9, 10, 61, 81
models/molds, 76–77
monasteries, 5, 6
money, 51–52
Mongols/Mongolia, vi, 12, 33, 81
moon, 85, 93–95
moon cakes, 81, 85
mountains, 7, 11, 49, 56
moveable type, 22, 25–28
moxibustion/mugwort, 67, 68
music, 97–101

N

*New Design for a Mechanized
    Armillary Sphere and
    Celestial Globe* (Su Song), 95
nomads, 2–3, 12, 33, 82
noodles, 80–81, 86–87
North China Plain, 6, 72
numbers, 108–115

O

octaves, 98
omens, 70

P

paddy fields, 73
palaces, vi, 6, 9–10, 93
paper, 16–21
papyrus, 16
pendulums, 105, 106
Periods. *See also* Dynasties
    Period of Disunion, v
    Spring and Autumn, iv
    Three Kingdoms, v
    Warring States, iv
pictograms, 23.
    See also calligraphy
pitch, 98
planets, 91–95

plows, 75
pollution, 7
population of China, 4
porcelain, 49, 102
printing, 22, 24–28
prisms, 44, 46
puppetry, 102–103

Q

qi, 11, 15, 66–69
Qin Dynasty, v
Qin Shi Huangdi (emperor),
    v, 9, 34, 50, 52
Qing Dynasty, 7, 10

R

rammed earth, 8, 9
relief maps, 56–57
religion, 91, 97
ri shun, 96
rice, 73
rivers, 7, 49, 51, 56, 72–73
roads, 14, 49–51, 53.
    See also Silk Road
rudders, 59–60

S

sailing, 58–62, 64–65
salt, 82–83
scales, musical, 98
seismographs, 52, 104–107
shamans, 98
Shang Dynasty, iv, 4, 6, 102, 109
Shen Nung (emperor), 84
Shennong, 69
shi, 69, 70
ships, 58–61, 64–65
silk, 34, 45–46
Silk Road, 6, 8, 50
silt, 73
Six-Cornered Snowflake, The
    (Kepler), 115
snowflakes, 114–115
solar calendar, 93, 94–95
Song Dynasty, vi, 62
Spiritual Constitution of the
    Universe (Chang Heng), 105

Spring and Autumn Period, iv
stars, 91–95
stern, 59
stirrups, 2–3, 32, 33
string instruments, 98, 99, 101
Su Song, vi, 95–96
Sun Tzu, *The Art of War*, 35
sunspots, 94
superstitions, 70
suspension bridges, 49, 50, 54–55
swords, 76–77
symmetry, 10–11

T

t'ai ch'i, 71
Tang Dynasty, vi, 102
tangrams, 109, 112–113
tea/tea ceremony, 84, 88–89
Temple of Heaven, 93
terracotta army, 34, 36–39
terrain, 56
theater, 100, 102–103
Three Kingdoms, v
Tien-Lcheu, 29
time, 94–96
to (bell), 97–98
toilet paper, 18
topography, 56
trace harnesses, 74, 77
trade, 9, 51–53, 82, 84.
    See also merchants
travel, 48–51. *See also* maps;
    roads; sailing
Ts'ai Lun, v, 17, 19

U

UNESCO, 9
unification of China, 49, 51

W

walled cities, 8.
    See also Great Wall of China
warfare, 30–35
Warring States Period, iv
water clocks, 95–96
weapons, 31–35, 44, 76–77
weaving, 44, 46

weights and measures, 51,
    52–53, 98–99
wheelbarrows, 76
wood, 10, 49, 56, 60, 96
wood pulp, 17, 18
wood-block printing, 24–25
World Heritage Site, 9
writing, 3, 18, 23–28.
    See also books

X

xi, 100
Xi'an, v, 5, 8, 17, 50
xingxing, 92

Y

Yangshao people, 72–73
Yangzi River, 7, 49, 73
yaw, 59
Yellow Emperor's Inner Cannon,
    The (Yellow Emperor), 67
Yellow River, 7, 72
Yi of Zeng, Lord, 99
yin and *yang*, 69–70
Yuan Dynasty, vi, 81
yurts, 12–13

Z

zajus, 100
zero, 110
zhen, 69, 70
Zheng He, vi, 61
Zhou Dynasty (Zhou kings),
    iv, 5, 85
zithers, 98, 99